Well, that ESCALATED QUICKLY

Well, That ESCALATED QUICKLY

Memoirs and Mistakes of an Accidental Activist

FRANCHESCA RAMSEY

GRAND CENTRAL
PUBLISHING

NEW YORK   BOSTON

Grand Central Publishing
Hachette Book Group
1290 Avenue of the Americas
New York, NY 10104
grandcentralpublishing.com
twitter.com/grandcentralpub

First Edition: May 2018

Grand Central Publishing is a division of Hachette Book Group Inc. The Grand Central Publishing name and logo is a trademark of Hachette Book Group, Inc.

The Hachette Speakers Bureau provides a wide range of authors for speaking events. To find out more, go to www.hachettespeakersbureau.com or call (866) 376-6591.

The publisher is not responsible for websites (or their content) that are not owned by the publisher.

Library of Congress Cataloging-in-Publication Data
Names: Ramsey, Franchesca, author.
Title: Well, that escalated quickly: memoirs and mistakes of an accidental
    activist / Franchesca Ramsey.
Description: New York: Grand Central Publishing, 2018.
Identifiers: LCCN 2017055221| ISBN 9781538761038 (hardback) | ISBN
    9781478999911 (audio download) | ISBN 9781538761045 (ebook)
Subjects: LCSH: Ramsey, Franchesca Television personalities—United
    States—Biography. | YouTube (Electronic resource)—Biography. | Bloggers—
    United States—Biography. | BISAC: BIOGRAPHY & AUTOBIOGRAPHY /
    Entertainment & Performing Arts. | BIOGRAPHY & AUTOBIOGRAPHY /
    Personal Memoirs. | BIOGRAPHY & AUTOBIOGRAPHY / Women.
Classification: LCC PN1992.4.R3573 A3 2018 | DDC 791.4502/8092 [B]—dc23
LC record available at https://lccn.loc.gov/2017055221

Printed in the United States of America

LSC-C

10 9 8 7 6 5 4 3 2 1

*For my mother, the best friend, best blessing,
and best role model a girl could ask for.*

CONTENTS

CONTENTS

Well, that ESCALATED QUICKLY

GIRL WALKS INTO THE COMMENTS SECTION

I know the exact date I went from being a nobody, minding my own business in my corporate retail job, to being "internet famous"—and inadvertently making a lot of girls cry.

I have a long and complicated history with the internet. I basically grew up online. I built my first website in middle school after spending the summer at computer camp learning how to code. My first boyfriend was a kid I met in an AOL chatroom. Smartphones and digital cameras didn't exist back then, so our late-'90s version of sexting was me taking a Polaroid of my nipple and scanning it. When I'm super famous and my long-lost internet boyfriend inevitably comes out of the woodwork and releases that photo to the press, I have a statement ready: "That low-res mess of pixels is not recognizable as a human breast."

In high school I bought my own domain name, franchesca.net, and started blogging about my life before it was actually called blogging. I kept that up through college before making the leap to video in 2006, one year after YouTube was founded. I spent the next six years making YouTube videos in my spare time, just for fun; the topics spanned everything from hairstyle tutorials to informational discussions about safe sex to original songs about student loan debt. (A sample: "Went off to school to get my education / Little did I know debt was part of the equation"—I know, I'm good.)

I'd spend hours each week filming and editing videos after work—and sometimes *during* work, when no one was paying attention—but I never had a very big audience. My comment section generally broke down into three categories:

---

1. "LOL"

2. "Kill yourself."

3. My mom scolding me about typos in graphics and inappropriate jokes

---

Then, one day, it actually happened—every YouTuber's not-so-secret dream: One of my videos went viral. And I don't mean *Huffington Post* viral. I'm talking supermassive, mainstream-news viral—an unstoppable contagion, if contagions also had some good side effects. It launched my career.

You could say it all happened because my high school's alumni Christmas party left me sick of white people's shit. I was frustrated by the same tired conversations I kept having with friends and acquaintances I had known for decades, the head patting, the hair yanking, and the gently racist observations that seem to just roll off the tongue after a few drinks. So I did the only thing I knew how to do moderately well: I put my frustrations into a video.

And before I knew it, my life got turned upside down, *Fresh Prince* style.

That video was "Shit White Girls Say...to Black Girls," and it was right on brand for the kind of social commentary I'd been begging people to watch on my YouTube channel and would soon be known for. Within a couple of hours of uploading "SWGSTBG," I was officially the new (sh)it girl. I soon quit my job to pursue acting and internetting full-time.

In the years since, a lot has changed. These days, most people know me as a fiercely passionate, outspoken social justice advocate, laying down truth on my MTV show *Decoded* or popping up as a commentator on cable news. But while I am extremely proud of the conversations my work has sparked around the world, I'm still embarrassed to admit that none of this was expected. Before my career exploded, I was pretty comfortable pushing pixels at my desk job as a graphic designer.

In other words, I didn't set out to be an activist, and I've made a lot of mistakes along the way. And precisely because of that, I think I have a lot to teach folks who find themselves on this same journey, struggling to find their voice and stand up for what they believe in without screaming at some guy who calls himself LethalDUMPS22 on Twitter that he doesn't know your life! Of course he doesn't know your life—he has chosen to go by the name LethalDUMPS22.

While I've never rocked a war bonnet at Coachella, I have put my foot in my mouth more than a few times. Social media means we're all living our lives in public now, and many of us are learning how to be advocates, allies, and activists in public, too. And while there may be nothing that can prepare you for the perks and pitfalls of being elected the "racism referee" among your friends and family, there are some proven methods for coping when someone writes a 1,500-word Tumblr post about how you are obviously oblivious to your self-hating racism. (The social justice glossary at the end of this book—"Franchesca's Simple Explanations of Not-So-Simple Concepts"—may also come in handy.) I've been on the receiving end of more than a few of those missives—and, I hate to admit it, have dished them out, too.

As the conversation about social justice broadens, I wish we could be more understanding of those who may be coming to it later than others. I was at a speaking gig at a university recently, and toward the end of the talk a girl in the audience asked me a question that made me really sad. She began by sharing that she felt guilty about how "ignorant" she had been in high school, where she'd been the only Asian student but had never thought about it much. Once she got to college, she started watching my videos, and now she couldn't get over all the times she hadn't objected to people's offensive comments, and times when she'd said disrespectful things herself. She ended by saying that she wanted to go back to her hometown and raise awareness at her high school, but she worried she would be hypocritical for doing so.

It can be really scary to admit that there are a lot of things you don't know. We live in a world where people are quick to pounce on you if you express confusion or ask a question, and many online activists aren't honest about the fact that they didn't always know what the gender binary was, either. Too often, people climb the ladder and say, "Hell yeah, I climbed the ladder! And I beat you to the top!" The thing about the ladder is that you never stop climbing, and if you think you have, you have a lot more work to do.

I told the "guilty" college student standing in front of me that I didn't even start thinking about this stuff until way after college, when a mob of angry Tumblr users descended on my social media accounts to explain to me exactly why I was a hopeless person who had no idea what she was talking about. I may not have always had the vocabulary to explain what I was talking about, but I was certainly not hopeless. My wake-up call didn't come until my twenties, and I'm still learning, too.

It can be hard to remember this today, when the stakes for these kinds of conversations are higher than ever. Because much of this work is happening online, especially for young people, the crucial nuances of face-to-face interaction are almost nonexistent. What's more, we now have a record of everything. It used to be that if you made a crass joke, someone might call you out on it, you could learn, and you could move on. But now these offhand, often accidental comments can be used as an indictment of someone's character in perpetuity. There are experts in the field of Problematic Archaeology who will spend hours combing through your tweets and preteen blogging efforts to uncover the most offensive artifacts of your past. (I've been those people—and I found what I was looking for.) Often, disagreements and misunderstandings escalate so quickly that there isn't time to reflect, understand where you went wrong (if you actually went wrong at all), and figure out how to fix it.

This book is an attempt to show you that mistakes are inevitable, and that what's actually important is how we use them to make a better world. For all the hate and abuse I get from all points on the political spectrum, I've been fortunate that many people have been compassionate about showing me where I messed up and helping me get back on track. I wanted to pay that generosity forward somehow, and I'm doing it the best way I can: by pulling my own receipts and dragging my former self.

CHAPTER ONE

FAMOUS IN FOUR HOURS

If I could do it all over again, I would have bought a better wig. The hair I wore to parody white girls was platinum blond, of course, and it hung a little past my shoulders in the kind of long layers beloved by women who star in reality TV shows set in California. In that way, it was perfect. But it also didn't really fit my head.

The morning before my life changed was like any other, except that I spent most of it looking at endless footage of myself in this bad wig. I'd set "Shit White Girls Say . . . to Black Girls" to upload to YouTube the night before; high-speed internet was a luxury I couldn't yet afford, and my connection was slow as hell. When I woke up, I saw that the upload had failed. Before I left for my job as a graphic designer at Ann Taylor, I started the upload again, thinking my hour-long commute would give it plenty of uninterrupted time to transfer and that I could finish the posting process from work. I looked at the still I'd chosen for the video: My eyebrows were halfway up my forehead, and my smile was cheesy. A few blond strands were caught on my hand, which was paused in the middle of raising the roof—part of my imitation of a white girl singing Nicki Minaj's "Super Bass." I didn't know it at the time, but millions of people were about to meet my freeze-frame face rocking this look.

When I got to work, I saw that my janky internet had pulled through. Our office had an open floor plan, which, while gorgeous and modern, was not architecturally convenient for maintaining a side hustle. As I edited my video's description box, I switched back and forth between YouTube and the image of Demi Moore in business-casual that I was Photoshopping for our new ad campaign, constantly looking over my shoulder to watch out for someone about to catch me in the act. "Ms. Ramsey...have you been producing humorous videos for the internet on company time?" (I have since accepted that procrastination is a fundamental part of any job requiring a computer.) I created a prewritten "Click to tweet" link, added all my social media links, and made sure to note the royalty-free music site I used for the end credits per instructions from Patrick, my then-aspiring-lawyer boyfriend. (Getting sued is one of my major career phobias.)

With the description box finished, "Shit White Girls Say...to Black Girls" was ready for her close-up. I changed the setting from private to public, and then, a full hour after arriving at work, finally decided to give Ann Taylor my full attention. I spent the morning listening to my *Hunger Games* audiobook and wielding my Magic Wand and Healing Brush on ladies in tasteful cardigans.

Before "SWGSTBG," I was convinced I was going to go viral for a parody video I'd made a few months before, "Student Loan Countdown." It was based on the criminally underrated Beyoncé bop "Countdown," and the idea for the parody came to me as soon as the original music video dropped. I worked around the clock to post mine in time to take advantage of the press already surrounding Bey. I stayed up all night writing lyrics; I went to American Apparel as soon as it opened to buy turtlenecks to match the ones she wears in the video; I spent hours tinkering with GarageBand to get my knockoff track to sound passable; and I exhausted myself learning Beyoncé's choreography and shooting multiple takes to get it exactly right. I got my parody up in twenty-four hours, which is some Beyoncé-level dedication, if I do say so myself. I'd worked hard writing and editing

"SWGSTBG," but it was nothing like what I did for "Student Loan Countdown," which generated about 100,000 views and was my most popular video ever. So I'd lowered my expectations. I thought "SWGSTBG" would do well, but for me that meant a couple hundred thousand views, maybe.

When lunch rolled around and I was able to pull myself away from the dual sagas of Katniss Everdeen and pleated slacks, I noticed my phone was buzzing a bit more than usual. My Gchats were blinking. My inbox was full of unread emails—sprinkled in with the usual YouTube comments were messages from Fox, the *Village Voice*, MSNBC, and the *Huffington Post*. Normally, when I made a video, I would spend an hour emailing blogs and media asking them to feature it. But I was at work, so I hadn't done any of that. Why were these people emailing me?

I typed "Shit White Girls Say to Black Girls" into Google, and there, at the top of the search results, was me, cheesing in that platinum-blond wig, next to one million views. I took a screenshot and pasted it into an email to my mom, my best friend De'Lon, and Patrick. Then I burst into tears. This was not a poignant, cinematic, twinkle-in-my-eye moment, but a sloppy, snotty, *my first boyfriend dumped me and we were SUPPOSED TO GET MARRIED* kind of cry. I don't know if it was the shock of it, or feeling overwhelmed because I had gone from no one watching my videos to, suddenly, everyone watching. It only took six long years and four incredibly fast hours. I was clutching my face, rocking back and forth, and mumbling, "Oh my God, oh my God," when a coworker came over and put her hand on my shoulder. "Is everything okay?"

I looked up at her. Where could I begin?

mmmmmmm

When "SWGSTBG" hit, I had no idea what going viral would entail, which I guess is why I burst into tears. Though I was working full-time, I barely made enough money to cover rent, bills, and my student loans. Patrick and I were living above an out-of-work opera singer whose erratic yet rigorous practice schedule meant my filming was often interrupted midmonologue by a burst of muffled eighteenth-century baritone. Once, I had to go down there at three a.m. to ask if he could please stop working on his Italian arias. He responded, "How did it sound, though?" While I've always been more of a lover than a fighter, it took everything in me to not slap him across the face and say, "It sounded like you need to shut the hell up." If he wasn't singing, he was fighting with his wife, who was upset that he was out of work. It was like my life was a sitcom about an aspiring actress in New York.

By that time, I had been making videos and posting them on YouTube for about six years. My first was a hair tutorial in which I explained how I put my hair up without a hair tie. The "secret" was taking two sections of locs and tying them into a bow. Very high-level stuff. The video was, to put it lightly, awful. To start, I was backlit, which is a total no-no. Always know where your light is, folks: in front of you. Then the tutorial hit a few snags when my narcissism got the best of me—"I'm trying to look at myself in the camera and I'm realizing it looks weird," I noted, aloud, about halfway through. But I persevered. I followed up that video with a blurry fifty-six-second clip of my dog Kaya jumping around on my bed to a heavy-metal soundtrack (chosen by Patrick). Soon I expanded my repertoire to making things people might actually want to watch, developed a little audience, and began devoting most of my free time (and much of my time on the clock at my day job) to YouTube.

Although I never had a specific goal, exactly, I knew I wanted to "work in entertainment" in some way. I'd racked up a nice chunk of student loan debt for half of an acting degree from the University of Michigan; after a few semesters taking classes on clowning, stage combat, and rolling around on the ground like a baby, I still had no idea how to break into the business, so I trans-ferred to the graphic design program at Miami International University of Art & Design.

After graduating, I didn't necessarily think YouTube was going to get me into show business. Back then, there was no formula for YouTube success because there was no such thing as YouTube success, no webcam-to-riches tales of network executives discovering sensations and offering them development deals. In 2008 YouTube launched its Partner Program, which gave people the opportunity to make money off the ads that played before their videos. After being denied twice, I was finally approved to participate and managed to make a little money from ads—I got a check for a hundred dollars every few months, if that. Though that's not to say I didn't see the potential. In 2008, right before I moved to New York in order to be close to auditions and agents, I won a contest to interview celebrities on the red carpet for the Emmys; this was the first of many times I was sure I was going to become famous and subsequently did not become famous. But really, YouTube was just a place to mess around, make stuff exactly how I wanted to make it, and meet people.

Especially after I moved to New York, posting videos on You-Tube was a way to scratch my performer's itch without having to claw my way through the city's stand-up scene. I didn't like to go out or drink; open mics were always late at night, and they usually paid in alcohol, if they paid at all. Because I lived in Queens, far away from the clubs downtown, I'd end up getting home at one or two in the morning before having to wake up at seven thirty for work the next day. Unlike most of the other comics I met, I couldn't work as a bartender or waiter because I can't even carry a single glass of wine across my living room without becoming a danger to myself and others. So I took odd jobs, like handing out club flyers and stuffing envelopes, in between working retail and graphic design temp jobs. Nevertheless, it was cool to be able to reach thousands of people on YouTube, rather than the same seven white dudes who frequented comedy clubs, and I liked being able to film multiple takes, especially when I had to pause for my neighbor's nightly opera performances.

In 2011 I thought for sure I'd gotten my big entertainment break when I entered YouTube's NextUp contest and, after two excruciating rounds of voting, managed to win. Along with twenty-four other YouTubers from around the country, I spent a week at the Google offices in New York City learning the ins and outs of YouTube and being mentored by some of the platform's top creators. We also got grants to invest in our channels. I spent most of the money on video equipment, including a new camera, computer, editing software, and lights, before putting the rest into savings and toward my hefty student loans. I decided this was my chance to get serious and make something out of my channel.

But even as I got more and more invested in my fans and my videos, in the real world I kept quiet about my YouTube jobby.* In those days, most people thought of YouTube as a place to watch videos, not make videos. Whenever I told people I had been making hairstyle tutorials and comedy videos for years, they would look at me as if I had just said something ludicrous, like "I dunno, I just don't think Lupita Nyong'o is THAT pretty." (*Who* would say this?!) YouTube was so new that many people didn't see the point in investing money and hours into a platform that was for movie trailers and cat videos. My friends from my performing arts high school didn't consider what I did "real acting," and although my family supported me, they didn't get it, either. When I told my grandmother, who doesn't have internet, that I made videos in my bedroom and posted them online—and that sometimes my boyfriend was in them—her response was "Do you have clothes on, Frannie?"

---

* Jobby = job/hobby.

Nevertheless, by the time the "Shit Girls Say" phenomenon hit in late 2011, I'd developed a voice and a dedicated audience of about ten thousand subscribers. If you somehow managed to not be one of the forty million people who watched the four-part "Shit…" series, I'll bring you up to speed. "Shit Girls Say" starred comedian Kyle Humphrey in drag, going through a series of quick scenes depicting stereotypical things "girls" say. When delivered in Humphrey's over-the-top upspeak and mashed together in a two-minute supercut, ordinary lines like "Do you know anything about computers?" and "Go into my purse…" and "Shut *UP*" took on a universal relatability. It went viral thanks to a perfect combination of "funny 'cause it's true," "dude in a wig," and "ha ha, girls are dumb."

As I watched the "Shit…" parodies pop up around the internet, I started to think about making my own. Then, about a week after the original video appeared, I got my inspiration from a video posted by stand-up comedian Billy Sorrells: "Shit Black Girls Say."

Well, sort of. As soon as the video began to play, Sorrells's portrayal of a stereotypical black girl named "Peaches" who liked blingy sunglasses and *Basketball Wives* made me feel weird. While the idea of a man in drag imitating the harmless things women and girls say has undertones of misogyny, in general "Shit Girls Say" felt lighthearted, all in good fun. I'm sure every person on earth, regardless of gender, has said, "Could you do me a favor?" at one time or another, and that's partially what made it funny. But the Peaches character felt different. Sorrells's dramatic, obnoxious black woman character seemed more like the butt of the joke than someone who was laughing along with it. There were also a few casual quips about domestic violence, as if that could ever possibly be funny.

Today, I know the vocabulary word to explain exactly why "Shit Black Girls Say" made me uncomfortable: *misogynoir*. The term, coined by activist Moya Bailey, describes the unique interplay of racism and sexism that black women face. Sorrells was drawing on an all-too-familiar trope: Black male comedians like Tyler Perry and Eddie Murphy donning drag and regurgitating the same racist stereotypes that white supremacy uses to oppress black women. These portrayals paint us as loud, angry, aggressive, hysterical, overly sexual, neck-swerving, gum-popping clichés who scream, "Oh, no, he didn't!" on loop. While these tropes persist all over modern media like Instagram, YouTube, Vine (RIP), and film and television, they're not too different from the mammy and Jezebel stereotypes promoted by Jim Crow–era advertisements and cartoons.

But at the time, I couldn't have explained any of this to you; all I knew was that I didn't relate. Like everyone else, I saw "Shit Black Girls Say" all over Facebook, and even a few of my coworkers were sending it around, laughing hysterically and exchanging *omg so true!*'s. (As the only black woman on my team, I found this particularly alienating.) The whole point of the "Shit…" meme was for audiences to see themselves in the character. But that wasn't my version of blackness; Peaches was like a cross between my high school bullies and Martin Lawrence's Sheneneh character. The more I thought about it, the more angry I got that this video might make my white coworkers and friends believe stereotyping blackness—and especially black womanhood—in this way was acceptable. As long as it's done by a black person, with a dose of humor!

If that's not me, I thought, *then what "shit" do I say?* I started to brainstorm ideas for my own take on the meme. I considered "Shit Black Suburban Girls Say," since I grew up in the suburbs, but that was too clunky. I toyed with "Shit Oreos Say," since that's what people used to say I was—an Oreo.* But my

---

* "Black on the outside, white on the inside"—I shouldn't have to explain why this is messed up.

fear of litigation stopped me there. What if Nabisco tried to come after me for trademark infringement? After racking my brain for days, I decided it was probably too late to make a spinoff of my own anyway.

That changed around Christmas. While home in Florida I went to my high school's annual holiday reunion. That year's party wasn't any different from those of years past, except that night I was driving, which meant I wasn't drinking. As the night went on, things got awkward, and I guess this was the first time I was sober enough to recognize just how much I put up with people treating me differently. I had shown up to the party with my locs (duh—they're attached to my head), which I hadn't had in high school, and as everyone around me got drunker, they became bolder. The usual questions about my hair, including "Is it real?" and especially "Can I touch it?" started to come out. And like most white people I'd ever talked to about my hair, these sloppy drunks already had their hands out, en route to groping my head, when they "asked."

I'm embarrassed to say that I didn't exactly stand up for myself when my friends started acting this way. I did my best to bob and weave as hands flew at me left and right, but I didn't have the courage to say outright, "Please keep your grubby fingers to yourself," or "Notice I'm not asking if your breasts are real because that's none of my business." Dealing with white people faux pas as a black woman is tricky: If you get upset, you can quickly be labeled the "angry black girl"; if you're too passive, it seems like you're giving permission, or letting racism slide. I had always been the token black girl in the group, so I knew this struggle well. Before I went natural,* I hardly knew anyone in real life with natural hair, let alone with locs, so I can see how my

---

* "Going natural" means transitioning one's hair to its natural texture after chemical straightening.

hair seemed new and strange to some of my friends. But curiosity doesn't give you free rein to treat me like a baby goat at the petting zoo. I know I'm just as cute as a baby goat, but back off.

The combination of this party and "Shit Black Girls Say" made something click. While part of me cringed, another part knew that this could be the makings of an incredible video. I whipped out my phone and started making a list of all the "Can I touch your hair?"–type comments I could think of. *You're not the same as other black people. He's so cute for a black guy! You can say the N-word, but I can't? You guys can do* so much *with your hair. It kind of feels like Cheetos! Is that racist? Is that racist? That's* NOT *racist!* An old friend, Megan, who was at the alumni party, provided the perfect inspiration for the nasal voice and the lazy way I waved that cigarette around in some of the scenes. As soon as I got back to New York, I called my friend with a fancy camera, Eric Walter, and got to work on what would become "Shit White Girls Say…to Black Girls."

* wwwwww*

Though many articles explaining "Here's What It's Like to Be a Viral Video Star" have been published over the last few years, in 2011 there was no handbook for what to do when you suddenly find yourself thrust into the spotlight. Sitting there in my cubicle, bawling my eyes out in front of my coworkers, I felt like the entire world was watching to see what I would do next. It was amazing to go viral for something I'd written and produced—a friend of mine had his first viral hit with a video of his mom sleepwalking, which is funny but not exactly what you want to be known for as a comedian. Still, all the attention was overwhelming.

The first of many unsettling realizations was that I still had to finish the workday. Sadly, YouTube does not show up at your office with one of those giant Publishers Clearing House checks, and though you may feel pretty proud of yourself, you are not immediately infused with the confidence to give your boss the finger and leave the office in a blaze of upwardly mobile glory. I wouldn't have done that anyway—I liked my job. Instead, I had to find some way to explain to the growing crowd of concerned coworkers gathering around me that I had been making YouTube videos for years, and finally one had gone viral. I felt like I was about to tell my spouse that I had a secret family, or confess that I liked to dress up in furry costumes and play with kitty litter in the bedroom.* My private hobby was about to become super public.

I knew my coworkers had seen "Shit Girls Say" and "Shit Black Girls Say," and although virality and internet fame were not the daily occurrences then that they are today, they were still concepts most people understood. *What's the worst that can happen?* I thought. I hadn't studied the Ann Taylor code of conduct nearly as closely as I should have (to say I skimmed it would be an overstatement), but I was pretty sure satire wasn't a firing offense.

I took a deep breath and said, "I made a response to that 'Shit Girls Say' video, and now it's going viral."

Kate, the most sophisticated of the bunch, was visibly surprised. "*You* make YouTube videos?"

Then, to my own surprise, Richard chimed in with, "What's that supposed to mean? I've made a few videos."

Jenna asked, "Well, can we watch it?"

You know how embarrassing it is when you show someone a video you think is really funny and they don't laugh? And you have to sit there as they watch the video on your phone, not laughing, waiting for the tense period of not-laughing to end?

As my coworkers crowded around my desk to watch "SWGSTBG," I envisioned their faces falling one by one as they tried to assure me, "Oh, yeah, it was really…something." After making hundreds of

---

* Neither of these is true of me, but no shame if you're a furry.

videos, I'd gotten over the discomfort and nervousness that came along with venturing into the comments, but seeing people I actually knew watch my work, in real time, was super uncomfortable.

The first thirty seconds felt like an eternity. Did they think it was funny? Did they think it was offensive? Jenna was a blonde—did she think this was about her? None of them had ever said any of the phrases in the video to me, but I couldn't be certain they hadn't said those things to anyone else. Maybe this wasn't a good idea after all. Was I ready to talk about race with my coworkers?

Finally, they started laughing. They got it! Maybe some of them would share it! (I stopped myself from chiming in with "Don't forget to subscribe!" when it was over—too thirsty.) Throughout the day they morphed into my own personal cheerleading section, yelling out to the whole office when one of their friends posted the video on Facebook. When it was finally late enough in the day that I could go home, Richard hugged me and said, "I can't wait to tell people we work together! Girlfriend!" He'd never called me "girlfriend" before. Had I just unwittingly opened an annoying door I could never close, or was it a harmless callback? I decided it was the latter and sank into the hug. This felt good. Maybe "Do I still have a job?" was written all over my face as I packed up, or perhaps the universe was just telling me to calm down, but either way, my supervisor, Jonathan, leaned over my desk and cooed, "Who knew we had a celebrity on our team?"

When I got home, my dogs, Fil (short for Filthy McNasty) and Kaya, hadn't gotten the memo that I was a star—they just wanted to go on a walk. I tried to use it as an opportunity to relax, but I couldn't stop scrolling through my phone. My inbox was flooded, my Twitter mentions were a mess, and I may have paused mid-poop scoop to check the view count on the video. It was a wonder we made it to the park and back without getting hit by a car.

I can hear the news story now: "Viral star struck and killed in Queens intersection while responding to 'y u so rassit?' tweet. More at eleven."

Back in my apartment I finally had a moment to reflect. On one hand, I felt like I'd finished a marathon—all the time I spent writing and editing my videos, tweaking them to perfection, staying up late, and waking up early was finally paying off in a way I could never have anticipated. On the other, it was like being bestowed a gift from the internet gods—my career was about to change in a major way, and the opportunity seemed like it had dropped out of the sky. I knew the old saying "There's no such thing as an overnight sensation," and I knew I had been building the foundation for this success for years. But like so many other viral videos, "SWGSTBG" went viral because of a precise combination of timing, hard work, and luck, and the luck part was trippy.

Before I could tackle my raging inbox, I had to take care of some family business. Though I still couldn't bring myself to say "shit" in front of her, I called my mom to fill her in on all the exciting emails and opportunities that were pouring in. She christened me "Miss Viral." Then, Patrick's mom, Nancy, called to congratulate me—and apologize.

The first time I met Nancy—who is, like Patrick, white—I had just spent the night with Patrick and was slipping out of the apartment they lived in together the next morning. Suddenly, I heard the front door open, and there was my boyfriend's mother, walking in from her night shift working as a nurse. Apparently Patrick had told her about me, because she said, "You must be Fran!" I'd recently added fire-engine red to my locs, which I thought was daring and cute but in retrospect probably made my hair actually look like Cheetos. After I'd sheepishly introduced myself, Nancy added, "Oh, I love your hair!" and extended her hand to give my locs a stroke. I was very clearly still wearing last night's makeup and rocking severe bed head* so there was no way to mistake what I'd been up to with her son the night before. I decided to not make the situation any worse, so I said thank you and made my exit.

After praising my performance in "SWGSTBG" on the phone, Nancy got serious. "Oh my God, Fran—I feel so terrible about touching your hair." I hadn't made the video to call her out, but I'd inadvertently done just that. I told her not to worry about it, but the moment made me realize how often I didn't tell people how I was actually feeling, especially if there was a power dynamic at play. I'd been dodging head pats and holding my tongue around coworkers, friends, bosses, and teachers for my whole life. Instead of saying something about how uncomfortable their comments or behavior made me, I'd channeled those feelings into a parody video. "SWGSTBG" brought to the surface how silent I had been—as a teenager growing up in West Palm Beach, as a young woman at college, and all throughout my early twenties.

Even before I fully grasped what the success of the video would mean for my life and my career, I realized it wasn't just about my hair. It was about growing up in Florida, where tanning is practically an Olympic sport, and having white girlfriends joke, "I'm blacker than you." It was about fielding comments that a certain man was "pretty hot for a black guy." It was about realizing that "I'm not into _____" is really code for "I see all _____ as the same." It was about not being "like other black girls" because I was "so nice" or "one of the good ones." It was about all the seemingly benign comments and expressions of disregard that added up to a constant reminder that I was different from other people, and that my difference was, for some reason, important. In many ways, being called "so nice" or held up as "one of the good

---

* Tip: If you think the date will go well, stuff a night scarf in your purse before you leave the house.

ones" becomes a kind of muzzle. Though I didn't know it at first, "SWGSTBG" was me taking off the muzzle. I'd found my voice.

As I scrolled through my inbox and social media accounts that night, it was really weird to see people from high school posting my video—did they not remember saying those things to me? Maybe they did, and they felt ashamed, or maybe they didn't and just wanted to get credit for knowing me. Producing a viral video has the strange power of elevating acquaintances to the level of "oldest and best of friends"—anyone who had direct access to me began reaching out. I got so many texts from random numbers saying, "Everyone on my Facebook is sharing your video!" that I was tempted to respond, "Same phone. Who dis?"

Meanwhile, every white girl I'd ever met decided to reach out to ask which lines were about her. I've never felt closer to Carly Simon in my life. ("You're so vain, you probably think this song is about you.") When a girl I'd worked with in Miami, who eventually did become a friend, texted to ask, "Tell me the truth. How many of those comments were from me?" I was completely honest: "I had to cut yours because it was so stupid I didn't think anyone would believe it." She responded with a string of cry-laughing emojis. The incident I was thinking of was the time she gave me a black shirt to wear to our company golf tournament because, "You know, you're black." And now you see why her comment landed on the cutting-room floor.

More importantly, I knew that my message was resonating with people who'd had to deal with the same awkward, inappropriate situations I did. The positive comments and emails and friend requests I received the day I went viral came from girls, boys, women, men, and everyone in between who had grown up just like me. They were the only person of color in all their high school and company photos. Like me, they'd been treated to bizarre throwaway comments for their whole lives. And like me, they hadn't known how to respond, so they didn't.

As much as I wanted to reply to each and every one of my new supporters, I had some media requests to answer. In addition to the *Huffington Post*, MSNBC, Fox, and the *Village Voice*, I got messages from *Saturday Night Live* and the team that would eventually become my talent agents. Producers from places like MTV, NPR, and *Anderson Live* were asking if I would do interviews or appear on their shows.

And they were asking if I would bring the wig. The principle of the wig still stood: It was an immediate signal about the theme of the video and the message I was trying to get across. Nevertheless, I always told them no. Though I still have that thing tangled up in a box in my closet somewhere, I knew I was destined to be more than the girl with the wig.

CHAPTER TWO

BLACK-LASH

The biggest audition I'd snagged in the first four years I'd been in New York was for the reality TV competition show *The Glee Project*, where twelve singers competed for a chance at a guest-starring role on the Fox musical comedy show *Glee*. Very high-brow stuff. Needless to say, I did not book the job. Despite occasionally getting carded at bars and taking karaoke way too seriously, I guess I wasn't believable as a teenage singing sensation on a should've-been-canceled-after-one-season Fox show.

But following "SWGSTBG," suddenly everyone wanted a piece of me—after years of celebrating anytime a casting breakdown said "open to all ethnicities," I had more interview requests, meetings with agents, and audition opportunities than I knew what to do with.

I tried to respond to as many as possible, which translated to leaving early for lunch to take calls away from my desk. At one point I volunteered to "help" one of my coworkers by accompanying her on an office coffee run just so I could take a call with my soon-to-be agent in the Starbucks restroom.

While radio and magazine interviews were exciting, nothing could prepare me for a message from *Anderson Live*, Anderson Cooper's daytime talk show, where he covered trending stories that didn't quite fit into his news beat at CNN. A producer from the show emailed me a few days after "SWGSTBG" blew up. My cue to "head to lunch."

I'd spent the past few days reading tons of articles about the "Shit Girls Say" meme, so I felt more than prepared to handle the producer's pre-interview spiel. Besides your usual "Where are you from? What inspired the video?" type of questions, we talked at length about the negative response to my jokes. Was I surprised people thought the video was "racist toward white people"?

I told her I wasn't surprised that people were upset or confused, but it was pretty revealing that no one had reacted negatively to the original video, "Shit Girls Say," which portrayed women as obnoxious, dumb, and preoccupied with trivial things. Or to "Shit Black Girls Say," which was basically just another rehash of the sassy black woman stereotype. Sure, they were supposed to be a bit over the top, but they didn't exactly present women, or more specifically black women, in a positive light. Apparently, I said, they had gotten a boys'-club pass. I'd seen little to no backlash against those videos. They certainly weren't being invited on national television to discuss the complicated politics of their two-minute satirical riffs on everyday interactions. I didn't quite have the language to express it at the time, but in retrospect I can see that the negative response to my video was a clear symptom of a racist and sexist culture that was viscerally offended by the idea of a black woman talking about her lived experience.

The *Anderson* interview looked like it was going to be a go. Then, right before we got off the phone, the producer asked if I'd invite the old friend on whom I'd based my "SWGSTBG" voice and mannerisms, Megan, to come on the show. I told her I'd give it a shot, but realistically I wasn't so sure it was an option. There's just no easy way to say, "Hey, would you be interested in going on national television to talk about all the dumb things you've said to me throughout our fifteen years of friendship?" But I must have done an okay job of it, because I called her up and she agreed—I'm sure the free flight from LA to New York, combined with Megan being an aspiring actress looking for screen time, didn't hurt. The night before the taping, I braided my hair, laid out the dress I planned to wear (it was from Target), and went to bed early. I was nervous but excited—I saw *Anderson* as a chance to put myself on the map.

My segment was only twelve minutes long, but the taping lasted more than half an hour. Anderson was warm, charming, and even more handsome in person. (For those wondering, yes, his eyes really are that blue. "Silver fox" is a total misnomer—dude straight-up looks like a wolf.) He joked with me between takes and complimented my poise and professionalism, which made me blush. Did I already mention how handsome he was? As I studied the way he read from the teleprompter and bantered with the audience, I knew I wanted to be where he was someday.

Aside from one strained exchange with an audience member, the experience went well. Even Megan seemed to be having a good time when Anderson pulled her out of the audience and we all laughed together about her nasal voice. I felt like I'd nailed it—which was good, because I had to run from the taping to a meeting uptown, where I officially snagged an agent.

~~~~~~~~~

In the week between taping *Anderson* and the segment going up, I had also been invited to audition for *Saturday Night Live*. This was nearly a year before the conversation about why there wasn't a black woman on *SNL* hit a fever pitch, but still: I knew there wasn't a black woman in the cast at the time, and I couldn't help thinking that maybe *I* could be the black woman on *SNL*. The audition invite didn't provide many details—just that those auditioning should prepare a character showcase—and my new agent, Scott, told me to "do four characters I loved."

Eager to support their brand-new client, Scott and a group of people from his team said they would come cheer me on. I had been watching the show for my entire life—you can't claim to want to be a comedian without spending some amount of time proclaiming, "Live from New York, it's Saturday night!" alone to your bathroom mirror. The opportunity was a dream come true.

More precisely, it was one of those dreams where you're onstage, you suddenly realize you're naked, and everyone starts laughing at you. But in my case, not many people laughed.

Almost as soon as I walked into the club, I knew I was going to bomb. The audition invitation had been vague because everyone else trying out was a UCB°-trained comic who had studied *SNL* auditions, which require a very specific kind of comedy, for years. They didn't need instructions. It had never even occurred to me to ask my agent for sample audition tapes or to look for audition videos on YouTube—you know, the very platform that had earned me an audition in the first place. (PSA: YouTube has tons of *SNL* audition tapes and screen tests from talented comedians who did and didn't make the cut.) To top it all off, I'd been working on my characters for about a week, and instead of trying out my routine beforehand in front of an audience at a comedy club, I opted for the acclaimed "Above the Opera Singer Theater," aka my living room. Patrick gave me some feedback, but getting one person's perspective is not the same as having an audience, especially when that one person is like Patrick and doesn't really know much about pop culture. As much as I love him, he once asked me if Selena was still alive, and I couldn't help but wonder, aloud, "Who the hell did I marry?" I hadn't performed stand-up since moving

---

* UCB is the Upright Citizens Brigade Theatre, an improv theater and training program founded by Matt Besser, Amy Poehler, Ian Roberts, and Matt Walsh. There are a number of improv comedy programs in New York, but UCB is seen as one of the big dogs because it's churned out a number of *SNL* cast members.

to New York, and YouTube comedy is completely different—you can edit the hell out of yourself to make sure all your jokes hit.

For my character showcase, I had come up with the idea that I'd be at an awards show and play both the presenter and the winners: Tyra Banks was hosting, and Lil Wayne, Britney Spears, my grandma, and Megan from "SWGSTBG" would be accepting awards. Not the most original pitch by any stretch of the imagination, but I figured it would get the job done. This was nothing like what the other comics had prepared. Instead of a generic, predictable location for their impressions, they'd introduce each character with an oddly specific, bizarre scenario—kind of like the premise of an SNL sketch: "This is Tom Hanks, who has stubbed his toe because he's been helping someone move," or "Here's Sofía Vergara as a real estate agent in New York." I can do a great Britney Spears impression, but I had no context for it. (Example: "Here's Britney Spears babysitting for a Russian diplomat!")

Out of twelve *SNL* hopefuls that night (including Sasheer Zamata, who did eventually join the cast), I was scheduled to go on eleventh, which made the whole thing more excruciating. Over and over, I watched people who were so prepared, so funny, and so on point that I wondered if my agent was going to drop me when I finally wandered onstage. Or if I should just get it over with and drop myself.

When my turn came around, I decided I needed to get through my performance as fast as possible. I introduced each character as Tyra Banks, praying the audience would get my basic *America's Next Top Model* references. "I only have one photo in my hand, and it's of Franchesca's grandma"; "I was rooting for you, Britney Spears! We were all rooting for you!" It was exactly as bad as I expected it would be. My performance was less professional comedy routine and more Twenty-Fifth Annual Dunder Mifflin Paper Company Talent Show. While I don't think I'll ever be right for *SNL*, I would totally place at DMPC. I swear my Britney is that good.

After the final comic finished, Scott and the rest of the group from the agency walked me to the subway. I was trying very hard to hold it together, but I was humiliated—not just because of my performance, but because I worried they thought I was lazy and unprepared. I hadn't even met some of them before, and I hated that this was the first thing they'd seen me do. Somehow, they didn't fire me, but as I made the hour-long trek back up to Queens, humbled and embarrassed, I realized I had let all the attention from "SWGSTBG" go to my head. I had worked for years honing my specific skill set, but that didn't mean I was an expert.

mmmmmm

Though the *SNL* audition was a bruise to my ego, I was able to bounce back for the airing of my *Anderson* interview. "SWGSTBG" was well past six million views, and despite a Lil Wayne impression that consisted of nothing more than an aluminum foil grill, shades, and a backwards hat, I still officially had an agent. I was getting called for auditions left and right, and my very first national TV interview was about to debut. I was glowing.

I didn't have access to a TV at work, so I was stuck reading tweets about the show as it aired instead of watching it live. I didn't have cable or DVR at home, either, so my friend Dominic recorded the episode and a group of us planned to watch it after work. I spent the entire day refreshing my timeline instead of Photoshopping statement blazers, and at five p.m. I sped out of the office like I had just been told there was an athleisure sample sale in the lobby. (What can I say? I love high-end sweatpants at almost affordable prices.)

That evening, I sat in Dom's tiny living room with Pat and our friends, drinking and eating snacks as if we were about to watch the Oscars. After Dom's grand introduction—"Tonight we're gathered to celebrate Fran because we love her and because we're all jealous she got to meet Anderson fucking Cooper!"—the segment began to play. My heart was pounding as suddenly I was on-screen in my platinum-blond wig, saying:

Not to sound racist, but you can say the N-word, but I can't?

My best friend was black—well, she's still black, but we're not really friends anymore.

Oh my God, I'm practically black! Twinsies!

This is so ghetto.

So cute for a black guy, right?

Can I touch it? Okay. I'm already touching it a little. Is this real? Wait, it's not real? It is. So nappy.

I think what I like the most about them is they're not, like, stereotypical, like, black people. You know what I mean?

It's almost like you're not black.

When the clip from "SWGSTBG" was over, we were transported back to the studio, where Anderson and I were sitting down for a one-on-one. While I certainly remembered being there, I almost couldn't believe how comfortable and professional I looked. My little black dress looked damn good, my hair was piled high in my expertly braided updo, and my eyes sparkled like your grandmother's favorite holiday shawl. I heard myself explaining how I thought the "Shit Girls Say" videos were funny, but I couldn't really relate to them. "Being a YouTuber," I was saying, "I thought, *How can I jump on this and get tons of views?* Because I want to get views, too—I'm going to be honest."

The audience laughed, and so did our living room viewing party. Seeing myself on television instead of on my computer screen was surreal. And I was pleasantly surprised to find that all the talk about the camera adding ten pounds was clearly bullshit.

Then Anderson got into the drama portion of the interview— the backlash to my video. Slowly, I began to look less poised. "Have you been surprised at the reaction?" he asked, in that Scholarly Dad voice he has. "Some of the comments online have said it's racist, what you've done."

I knew this was coming, and I had practiced my answer before the taping. "Well, I think to be fair, my intention was not to label anyone as a racist, because in all honesty, none of those comments are actually racist."

If you're thinking: *Wait a second, 2012 Franchesca. Those comments AREN'T racist? They're as racist as a "12 Reasons Obummer Is a Kenyan Muslim" novelty calendar!*—well, so were a lot of people. I'll get to that in a second.

I went on to explain that curiosity was totally understandable, but treating black women like they were animals at a petting zoo was not. "I think a lot of times people are trying to relate to me and show me that we're cool and we can get along," I said. "They're trying to be nice, but then the wrong thing slips

30

out." It's almost funny to look back at how conciliatory and non-confrontational I was being. How could anyone be offended by that?

Anderson took a few comments from black women in the audience, and they said the video was a great icebreaker for racial dialogue with their friends and coworkers. They found it relatable and funny and were happy to share it with their friends. Awesome. But then, Anderson approached an older white woman in the audience. Back at Dom's apartment, I rolled my eyes—I already knew how this exchange played out.

> **Salty Lady:**   Hi. I was just wondering, if you say it had no racism or connotations, why do you use white and black girls? Why didn't you just say, you know, "Funny Things Stupid People Say to Me" rather than using the black and the white?

> **Me [visibly annoyed, to some laughter in the audience]:**   Okay. Once again, the original video...

As I watched my eyebrows rise higher and higher into my perfectly sculpted updo, I felt like I was about to crawl out of my skin. *Let me not be the "angry black girl" on national TV!* I thought. Even though I had every right to find this woman's comment infuriating—had I not just explained the concept minutes before?—I was projecting the stereotype onto myself.

She kept going:

> **Salty Lady:**   Saying black and white is what I'm getting at.

> **Me:**   I know. I'm going to answer your question. The original video that this is based off of is "Stuff Girls Say."

Then the most popular parody of that video was "Stuff Black Girls Say." So my idea...

Anderson cut in to ask if I had been offended by the previous "Shit Girls Say" videos. I assured him that no, I hadn't, and was about to explain further when my number one fan cut in again.

Salty Lady: I feel like white people are the only people that can be racist.

Me [obviously exasperated]:   Nothing said in the video is racist. Honestly. I mean, asking about my hair, saying that you think someone is attractive despite being black— I don't think any of those statements are racist. I do think that they are ignorant. I mean, I really am sorry if people are offended or they are upset about it, but I think that if you don't see anything of yourself in it, then I don't think it should be offensive.

Though I did do an admirable job of replacing every single "Shit" with "Stuff" for daytime audiences, I was starting to feel bad about how I looked on TV. On top of the tense back-and-forth, the way the segment had been edited made me look bored and nervous as I sat listening to the audience's questions and comments. I'd been on TV before, but only local news ("Florida girl wins contest to go to the Emmys"), and the *Anderson* segment involved more production than I could have expected. Now, having worked on TV, I don't think it was malicious—you've gotta get that B-roll.* I learned an important show-biz lesson that day:

---

*   B-roll is the footage editors splice into the main shot in order to make a segment look more dynamic. Think static images of an interviewee's face, or shots of the scenery. I didn't know about B-roll, so when the focus was off me during taping, I let myself go into resting bitch face.

As dubious as the name may be, "resting bitch face" is real, and it's the stuff of TV magic. But at the time, I felt a little manipulated. Patrick shot me a confused, angry look. Was this about to go south?

"Ugh!" Dominic said. "That lady was so obnoxious. More power to you—I would've told her off. Seriously, sit down!"

I tried to go back to the segment, which had moved on to man-on-the-street interviews about the video. Most reactions were positive, with lots of black women agreeing they'd heard the statements before, and even a few white women agreeing that the comments were commonplace. Then the segment reached the last young woman.

Carnival Pretzel–Level Salty Girl: By doing it, she's being racist to me.

It was like I had been transported back to that exact moment and was reliving it in real time. How could she think that me talking about my (very benign) experiences as a black woman was racist? And how did I not scream in the studio the minute she pulled the reverse racism card?

Anderson: It's interesting. Franchesca, you heard that last young woman saying that you were being racist to her.

Me: I don't think that talking about ignorance is racist. Like I said, I'm not labeling anyone racist, because that would imply that the statements were saying that someone is better than another race, and that's not what any of the statements are doing.

After the commercial break, we got to the portion with Megan, and my friends began laughing it off and chatting among themselves.

But I couldn't stop going over my responses to Anderson's questions. Actually, maybe saying someone is "so cute for a black guy" *does* imply racial superiority of some kind, right? Using "It's almost like you're not black" as a compliment lumps all black people together, and it suggests they're generally worse than white people. Working through the whole thing felt too complicated to explore in a twelve-minute TV segment, so I told myself to let it go. Even though I can see now where I messed up, I had done pretty well for a girl who'd had no publicist, no agent, no manager, and only a pep talk from her boyfriend and dogs to prepare.

But not everyone was willing to give me so much credit. Or any credit. At all.

ⅿⅿⅿⅿⅿⅿ

If I could go back in time, I would say, with confidence, "My video is not racist because I genuinely do not believe that racism against white people exists. Nothing I say or do could ever oppress white people, and my video certainly has not led to the oppression or mistreatment of white people. It might hurt some feelings, but this video isn't about hating white people. It's not about hating anyone. It's shining a light on the experiences black women and people of color face every single day in a world that says we're less than or 'weird' because we aren't white. And if that makes you uncomfortable, maybe you should consider whether the problem lies with you, not me."

Instead of a time machine, I had Black Tumblr.

If I thought my inbox was bad when I first went viral, it was even worse after my *Anderson* interview aired. A whole new wave of emails, messages, and comments crashed into every social media platform I was on. (Basically all of them.) As the days went on, the comments got more and more vitriolic—it was like my haters were taking time to build the perfect nasty insult.

People of all races—or who claimed they were of all races—were calling me names: the N-word, Uncle Tom, slur after slur after slur. I was devastated, and I couldn't understand it.

Before "SWGSTBG" went viral, I prided myself on being super engaged with my modest fan base, so my YouTube account was set to forward any comments on my videos to my email inbox; I wanted to be able to respond to comments in real time. Now that I was the new face of "reverse racism," thousands of hateful comments came straight to me, unfiltered. Although I eventually turned off my email notifications, for months I answered angry comments regularly. I was just so surprised by the backlash that I thought I could reason with people.

From one side, there was the conservative white supremacy stuff: I was a racist who hated white people and I should go back to Africa. Having grown up in a fairly diverse and liberal community, I'd never been called a racist before, and I was not prepared. I opted for the *kill them with kindness* approach: "I don't hate anyone, but I'd love to visit Africa someday! Thanks for the encouragement! ,)"

Eventually I forced myself to ignore the barrage of racist ramblings—a lesson I would return to over and over again in my career. But the criticism from the other side—from the left—was harder to disregard.

I'd been on the microblogging site Tumblr for a few years, steadily building a loyal audience by posting my hair tutorials and comedy videos and by reblogging viral content and occasionally adding personal commentary or jokes. After keeping a journal throughout high school and college, and abandoning LiveJournal when it was taken over by tweens, moving to Tumblr was a logical next step for me. The site served as a collaborative digital scrapbook—the community was just as much of a draw as the ease of publishing. It took all the work out of finding an audience of like-minded people with similar interests, and the site allowed microcommunities, ranging from fan fiction writers to conspiracy theorists to natural-hair bloggers, to proliferate.

Among these groups, Tumblr is probably best known for its active social justice community; it's a particularly good platform for marginalized folks to organize, vent, and boost news stories about race, gender, sexuality, mental health, and disability that would otherwise be ignored. When "SWGSTBG" went viral, I unwittingly attracted the attention of this community. They rallied behind me when Perez Hilton reuploaded the video without permission on his site (which lost me views, and money). They also used the video as a jumping-off point for lengthy discussions about the dangers of unchecked white privilege, power dynamics in majority-white spaces, respectability politics, and microaggressions. But as Tumblr users unpacked the issues, I was nowhere to be found—I was busy imagining my life as a celebrity, complete with a late-night comedy show gig and an extensive new wardrobe.

While I was riding high from my *Anderson* segment, my newfound Tumblr audience wasn't impressed. Why hadn't I shut down the woman who accused me of being racist toward her? Why hadn't I explained that racism against white people doesn't exist because there's no social structure oppressing white people? Why didn't I explain the concept of white privilege? Why had I said none of the comments in my video were racist when they clearly were? Why had I not used my new national TV platform to define the term "microaggression" for the masses? How did I not know about microaggressions? How dare I express sympathy with some of the people who'd been hurt by my video? How dare I have a white boyfriend? How dare I be so stupid?

I was used to white people saying they were upset by or didn't understand my video, but these messages were coming from black people, some of them even from academia. I was transported back to my middle and high school days, when my black peers would tell me I wasn't being black in the right way, that I "sounded like a white girl" or wished I were white. To hear Black Tumblr tell it, I had bombed *Anderson*, and no amount of praise from my agents or parents—or especially from my white boyfriend—was going to change their minds. I knew I'd started a conversation, but only then did I realize I'd suddenly been handed a gigantic platform to talk about race. It was becoming painfully obvious that I was far from prepared. I hadn't understood how much "SWGSTBG" meant to the people who felt they needed it most, and to them, I had fumbled the opportunity to turn it into something bigger than just a viral video.

The backlash, or *black-lash*, as I started to call it, came to a head when I posted a video sent to me by a white fan. Titled something like "Why 'Shit White Girls Say to Black Girls' Isn't Racist," the clip consists of a twenty-something white guy explaining power dynamics, institutional racism, microaggressions, and the fallacy of "reverse racism"—basically everything Black Tumblr had wanted me to say on my *Anderson* appearance. I thought it was a perfect breakdown that, in a tight five minutes, gave voice to things I'd captured in the video but hadn't been able to quite put into words. So I posted the video on Tumblr, adding a "disclaimer": The video repeated things black people have been saying for ages, but the sad truth was that some people would only listen if they were coming from a white person.

Wow. This, too, was the wrong thing to do. More than a few people responded that a white "translator" shouldn't be necessary for people to understand the issue. I agreed, but did so while holding my ground. I wrote a response on my Tumblr: "This shouldn't be an 'us vs. them' situation. The fact is that some people will refuse to digest the original message simply because it's coming from a person of color... Call me an idiot if you'd like, but I don't see how supporting someone (regardless of race) whose goal is to educate others deserves a side eye."

I shared this and sat back to wait for cookies and agreement for my excellent points. Instead, I got called out, in posts like "Chescaleigh, sit the fucking fuck down":

> This here is when I lay a big ass smack down on white-identifying wannabe cracker motherfucking ass...First, you ain't white. I know you wanna be chile, but you're not... You think whitey gonna see any different? HELL to the no. They see you as a N. I. G. G. E. R. PERIOD. Don't for a minute doubt that white people don't see your black ass as a straight up niggerrrrr...It's not "unfortunate" that some white people will refuse to take an anti-racist message from a person of color. IT'S RACIST, you racist apologist shitstain on the pants of fucking life...Seriously, what the fuck do you think happened on the Anderson show? White people set you up to be browbeat and shit on. And while I had no problem with you taking it because hey, it's a show, it's something, you actually ate their shit. In a fucking shit pie, served to you, and now you're vomiting it all over everyone, including your now EX-supporters.

I was absolutely crushed. I cried for what felt like an eternity. But instead of logging off, I went down the rabbit hole, hoping to find a way out. As I read every message, comment, and reblog trying to figure out where I'd gone wrong, I felt like my computer was going to burst into flames. I'd fallen into "callout culture"—as quickly as I'd become internet famous, I was in danger of losing the trust of the audience I'd built with those two minutes and thirty seconds of satire. I was ripped to shreds because I didn't know what I didn't know during my *Anderson* appearance, and now I was being ripped to shreds because I didn't know how to respond to being ripped to shreds. I'd gone from confident viral-video-star Franchesca to the high school version of myself—insecure, uncertain, and trying to balance my true self with the woman the world, and especially other black people, wanted me to be. I had just started to shake off the silly "racist" label from trolls and confused white people. But how could I shake off being a "coon" to the very black people who had, just days before, championed me for telling their stories?

I thought I was hot shit for making a viral video, but it was becoming clear that I had a lot to learn if I wanted to get to Anderson Cooper status someday. This is not an arena where you want to wing it, but I was not ready to be thrust into the role of activist and spokesperson. Like at my *SNL* audition, I hadn't even realized there was something to wing.

Though many of the commenters were totally off base, some of them had a point. There was no reason to prioritize a white voice in a conversation about black experiences. And while sarcasm and passive aggression made me feel superior to the trolls who slung personal insults and racial slurs, there was no place for it when interacting with people who called themselves fans.

One of the only reasons I didn't collapse into a puddle of hopelessness after the one-two punch of my failed *SNL* audition and incurring the wrath of Black Tumblr was that not everyone was calling for me to be permabanned from the cookout. A few black women reached out with some constructive criticism. They sent me reading lists and invites to private Facebook groups, and suddenly my Tumblr dashboard was filled with blogs like *Fuck-Yeah-Feminists!*, *POC Creators*, *Colorlines*, *Racialicious*, and *Racism-School*, which is basically exactly what it sounds like—a primer on all the concepts I'd experienced all the time but had never heard of. My eyes were being opened to new ways to talk about race, the media, and politics. I was starting to feel like I was back in school again, but for a different reason: I was cramming. I wanted to learn as much as I could as fast as possible, not only for myself but because all of a sudden people were coming to me for advice, and asking me for answers I didn't have. Soon I realized that my great talent lay in what I'd been doing, accidentally, in "SWGSTBG" and for years on YouTube: I had a knack for explaining things with jokes and pop culture.

Somehow, my agency didn't drop me after I bombed *SNL*, and it was really cool to realize that the team believed in me and saw my potential. (It helped to remember that Scott had no interaction with Black Tumblr, so he had no idea there was a corner of the internet that believed I should be banned from speaking publicly ever again.) And while it was becoming painfully obvious that I needed to proceed with caution, I now had the support of new online friends and mentors I could vent to and ask for support.

Meanwhile, at my day job, I was sneaking around so much that I felt like I was trying to hide an affair. Thankfully, my manager didn't really care that I was balancing my new life as an activist/actress with my full-time job; I always managed to get my work done on time and had no problem staying late to finish projects. Nevertheless, I quickly realized that if I wanted to take advantage of all the opportunities in front of me, I would have to quit. My boss didn't seem surprised when I told him I needed to resign, but I couldn't help but cry—I really liked the job, and I had just discovered the beauty of my employee discount. I'm not sure why, but people really sleep on Ann Taylor and their sister store, Loft. I'll admit I wasn't hip to it until I worked there myself, but now let me pass this totally not-sponsored good word on to you: Both brands have cute work and casual wear and bomb accessories, their shoes go up to size 11, and while most people know them as petite-friendly brands, they also carry tall sizes and go up to women's size 18. Now do you understand why I cried so hard?

While I didn't have a job to fall back on, I was able to quit because, soon after this whirlwind of a month, YouTube sent me a huge check—about $30,000 initially, and then $15,000 more after the popularity of "SWGSTBG" sent traffic to some of my other videos. I had no idea people were making that kind of money on YouTube—and neither did my bank teller.

When I went to deposit the first payment at my local branch, a little giddy, a little terrified that the check would somehow disintegrate in my hand between the front door and the counter, the man working asked, "Whoa. Why is Google giving *you* this much money?" It didn't register at the time that I probably should have interpreted this as a backhanded compliment, if not outright racist—I was wondering the same thing myself. Instead of asking to speak to the manager, or just getting a new teller, I asked him if he'd seen the viral YouTube video "Shit White Girls Say... to Black Girls," and explained that my check was payment for the ad views my video had racked up. He admitted to somehow missing the "Shit Girls Say" craze. I whipped out my phone so we could watch right there at the counter.

Thankfully, he laughed. Although it was a small thing, it gave me some much-needed perspective. Since the nesting dolls of controversy had taken up residence on my desk, my life had felt like it was taking place in the computer, in angry blog posts and furious messages. Getting a chuckle out of this random guy reminded me that my audience wasn't just made up of the most vocal or most online people. Reaching local bank employees was just as important as reaching Tumblr influencers, and slowly but surely, I was developing the vocabulary and confidence to have important conversations with both.

CHAPTER THREE

MY REIGN AS YOUTUBE'S CALLOUT QUEEN

It's impossible to be part of the YouTube community and not be at least familiar with Jenna Mourey, the vlogger better known as Jenna Marbles. The OG "queen of YouTube," she has more than seventeen million subscribers and a life-size wax figure at Madame Tussauds. One of her first videos, "How to Trick People into Thinking You're Good Looking," got over five million views in the first week she posted it; you might also know "How to Avoid Talking to People You Don't Want to Talk To" or "Drunk Makeup Tutorial." Her sense of humor is self-deprecating and punny, but she often mixes in a somewhat feminist message. ("Trick People" was a pretty biting—if occasionally casually offensive—commentary on the ridiculous beauty standards society holds for women.)

"Things I Don't Understand About Girls Part 2: Slut Edition," which Jenna posted in December 2012, was different. Off the bat, the tone was a little more bitter, a little more "I'm about to *say some things*." Filming in her dining room, with her familiar Spider-Man poster behind her, she begins with a disclosure: The video "isn't going to be that funny." Instead, she says, it's going to be "questions that I have for sluts."

She tells her viewers they should feel free to disagree with her and sound off in the comments. Then, she proceeds to aggressively attack women who have "a lot of casual sex." She goes on and on about one-night stands, which she does not understand because they put women at risk for getting "murdered and herpes." She criticizes a subcategory of sluts that she calls "stupid sluts" and suggests that women who have a lot of casual sex don't deserve respect, making a particular note that sluts who fuck other people's boyfriends are just "asking for it." Etc. It's almost ten minutes long.

Obviously, there are a lot of problems with this video. The whole premise, for starters. And are women in committed relationships somehow immune from violent crime or sexually transmitted infections? Several feminist YouTubers took Jenna to task for her textbook sex-negative slut-shaming. They did an awesome job of explaining the nuances of how the language Jenna used to denounce "sluts" was exactly the same as the language people use to silence sexual assault survivors and promote the centuries-old sexual double standard we all know and hate. They never attacked her, or said she was a despicable person for making the video. They just calmly explained where she'd gone wrong, why it was wrong, and what she could have done better.

When I watched the video, I was disappointed, and I couldn't shake the overwhelming sense of dread that one of her very first comments—about how engaging in "risky behavior" like one-night stands can lead to getting raped or murdered—had made me feel. But when I saw what Jenna's followers were commenting on the video, my shock and sadness turned to anger: People were agreeing with her, and many of them seemed young or impressionable. They wrote that they knew women who had been raped and were indeed huge "sluts." Others commented that they had been assaulted, and that this video had opened their eyes to what they should have done differently.

I contemplated diving into the comments, but instead I decided to make a response video because I thought I could contribute something unique to the conversation—a personal experience. In

"How Slut Shaming Becomes Victim Blaming," I told half a million people the story of how I "lost" my virginity. In reality, I did not misplace my virginity—I know where it went. A girlfriend got me concert tickets for my eighteenth birthday, and I spent the day leading up to the show drinking, feeling pressured by the group of older guys we were with. By the time the concert was over, I was wasted, and I passed out. It wasn't until the next morning that I realized I'd been, in the words of my giggling girlfriend, "soooo bad"—I'd "had sex" with one of the guys we were with, her boyfriend's older roommate. I remembered none of it, and I couldn't stop feeling guilty about how I could "let" myself be date-raped. I begged my friend, who was also my coworker at Blockbuster Video at the time, not to tell anyone we worked with about it. She immediately told everyone, including my manager, and they didn't handle it with discretion at all—they let me know they thought I was a huge "slut." On top of trying to deal with the trauma of being raped, I was totally humiliated. I couldn't afford to quit, so I asked to be moved to a different store and tried to put the whole thing behind me.

I never thought I'd tell that story on the internet. For one thing, I had only ever told my husband, Patrick—I had to call my mom before I posted the video to prepare her for it. Plus, I was still struggling to brand myself as an actress and comedian, and there is nothing funny about this story. I'd quit my graphic design job to focus on acting and writing full-time, but I was still living off my "SWGSTBG" money, since I wasn't booking many gigs. I worried about what my new agent would think.

But I knew that coming forward would be worth it if my story helped just one person. By the time Jenna released her video, I'd gone to therapy, worked through what happened to me, and finally recognized that it was not my fault, but the process had taken a long time. If I had seen Jenna's video soon after my rape, I don't know how I would have dealt with it. For many young women, Jenna is the pinnacle of coolness and success—something to aspire to—and I believed that if her thoughts on "sluts" were allowed to float around unchecked, they would cause harm.

Any nerves I felt about calling out a YouTube celebrity—the most famous woman on YouTube, really—dissipated when I thought about all the women who might see my response and feel less alone. Though I was nowhere near Jenna's level of fame, people were starting to see me as someone who had it all figured out. And I was careful not to attack or blame her—I just thought that talking about my experience could show people what it actually means to be a survivor of sexual assault. The truth is, it can happen to anyone.

In turn, I learned what it actually means to come out as a survivor of sexual assault. When "Victim Blaming" went viral, I got a lot of positive responses, and I never doubted my decision to tell my story—people sent messages saying the video had helped them gather the courage to press charges against their rapist or talk to their children about consent. But I also saw firsthand how our culture shames survivors who tell their stories. Jenna's fans were brutal—they said that I was just jealous of her and that I was racist (because of "SWGSTBG"), racial slurs were sprinkled throughout my comments, and folks argued that I had somehow ruined the life of the man I was "accusing of rape" even though I hadn't named him. (I don't even remember his name.)

I'd hoped that after I spilled my guts, Jenna would see the light and apologize. Maybe my video—combined with the other responses—could be a teachable moment for her. Maybe she'd respond to the criticism with a "Heal the World"–style musical apology starring various YouTube celebrities and donate the iTunes proceeds to RAINN.

She didn't do any of that. In the immediate aftermath, she silently removed the video from her channel and posted a condescending Facebook status about how people needed to learn to take a joke. She'd opened her video by encouraging differing opinions, but it was clear she wasn't interested in hearing anything other than "lolol sluts." In a *New York Times* interview about a year later, she said she'd been "crucified" for it.

That sucked, but whatever. I hadn't made my video for Jenna, anyway; I'd made it for her young fans. Though I had to endure a racist, sexist backlash (which, as you can tell, quickly became way too familiar to me), I knew I'd contributed something positive to the conversation. And it was a reminder that doing the right thing is hard and sometimes doesn't have the outcome you expect, or want.

I thought that was that, and I moved on. Then, three years later, I got a suspicious email through the contact form on my website. I thought it was someone trolling me, which happens a lot, especially when it comes to my more controversial videos. But I asked around and figured out the email really did come from who the sender said she was. It was Jenna Marbles, writing to apologize for the way she handled the situation, and to thank me for having the courage to call her out and tell my story.

wwwwww

I'd had a lot of experience with what we now know as callout culture after the *Anderson Live* appearance. But the situation with Jenna Marbles was the first time I got attention for being the caller and not the unsuspecting person picking up the phone. Though strangers who can't spell send you vile, insulting messages no matter whose side you're on, it was obviously a very different experience to be the referee.

Instead of shying away, I decided to dive in. Because I wasn't working regularly, I spent a lot of time on Twitter, Facebook, Tumblr, and YouTube, and although I wouldn't say I went looking for stuff to get mad about, I was more likely to chime in on trending stories or wade into comment sections to tell someone why what they said was racist, sexist, ableist, homophobic, transphobic, classist, or otherwise absolutely not okay. Eventually people started telling me I should comment on certain issues, sending me bigoted or prejudiced posts and asking if I'd heard about some awful thing so-and-so had said.

Whenever I got involved—which was often—I felt like I had to. Because no one else was, or because no one with an audience was, and I wanted to use my newish success for good. It felt like an uphill battle, but one I genuinely thought was worth it. I developed such a reputation as a callout queen that people began acting like it was my job—I became the go-to girl for defending marginalized people from bigotry, the final leg in the internet's racism relay. Posted a "comedy" sketch about slave rape? I was coming for you. An eight-minute video complaining about diversity and HIV testing? Please hold while I charge my camera batteries. In the habit of dropping the N-word and donning blackface and never seeing repercussions? Until now! I didn't care how many subscribers you had or how beloved you were, I was happy to put my SEO* skills to work and dig up your oldest, most racist videos, screencap them, and set them free like an injured bird I'd nursed back to health that was now ready to fly. It was cool to have an online identity and to be praised for it, and although the onslaught of abuse from my adversaries' fans often left me shaking and crying in front of my computer, I would always get an adrenaline rush out of it. I felt like I was changing the world—or at least the internet—for the better.

The first time I realized that I might have been misplacing my newfound social media power, if not using it for outright evil,

---

    *   *SEO* stands for "search engine optimization," and it refers to strategies websites use to make their posts show up near the top of search results; reverse-engineering SEO can help you unearth articles and videos that may have been buried over time.

came a few months after the Jenna Marbles incident. A man claiming to be named Andrew Moskowitz posted a Facebook comment on a *New York Times* article about racist hiring practices; claiming to be a hiring manager, Moskowitz wrote that he threw away a résumé if it had a name like Tamisha on it. On Twitter and Tumblr, people were enraged, and they took it upon themselves to get him fired from his job. But first, they had to find out where he worked.

Someone on Twitter started saying he worked at the Monroe Cotton Mills in Monroe, Georgia. The evidence? Well, Sherlock, he'd checked into the company on his Facebook page, so clearly they were mailing out his W-2. Not to mention that the idea of a racist working at a former cotton mill was almost poetic. With the company name in hand, everyone began bombarding the Monroe Cotton Mills with emails demanding action against Racist Andrew. Meanwhile, other users had confused the Monroe Cotton Mills with the nearby Cotton Warehouse and began sending *them* similar messages, as well as posting negative reviews on the business's Yelp page. The managers of both companies were perplexed.

"I have NEVER heard that name until 11 AM this morning, when I started getting emails sent to me during church asking why I hired a racist," one manager told the *Daily Dot*. "I have no idea where this guy works," the other manager said.

The Mills/Warehouse confusion was quickly quashed, but no one was willing to believe that the vigilante anti-racism force we'd assembled was mistaken and Moskowitz didn't work at either place. I, too, thought something fishy was going on, so I called the Monroe Cotton Mills and, in my best Southern belle accent, asked to speak to Mr. Moskowitz. The receptionist told me that although he wasn't there when we called, Andrew Moskowitz did work for the company and would be in on Monday. Got him!

When people suggested that maybe we should lay off until we had more information, I confidently replied that I had called the company and confirmed Moskowitz did work there. I continued: The manager of the Cotton Mills was probably just attempting to cover up their racist mistake by saying Moskowitz didn't work there, so we should call back on Monday, when he'd be in the office. After who knows how many people called his office and screamed at this receptionist for her duplicity, someone finally figured out that she worked for an answering service, not the Cotton Mills, and was required to answer any inquiry with "He's not in right now, but he can get back to you some other day." We had wasted not only our time and energy, but the time and energy of a bunch of innocent small-business employees.

mmmmmm

I was embarrassed, but the drama was addicting. Even when it backfired, I thought it ultimately generated more awareness of important issues. At the end of the day, wasn't I doing this for the issues?

In retrospect, I'm pretty sure some of the people I spent hours calling out on Twitter were baiting me. Many YouTubers and "internet personalities" have made careers out of getting their audiences to join out-of-proportion controversy, and I fell for it more times than I'd like to admit. Last year, I found a post on the *Daily Stormer*, the white supremacist message board that was instrumental in organizing the Charlottesville Unite the Right rally, that detailed how easy it was to troll me. There were screenshots featuring me going back and forth with racists, try-ing to reason with them and getting madder and madder. It was a wake-up call. There are people whose Twitter feeds consist entirely of antagonistic @-replies that they send to random peo-ple until someone bites. This is a game to them. They want you to waste your time on them instead of having productive conversations with people who matter.

I was always calm and reasonable when I presented my points, but it didn't matter—each time, I was inundated with abuse, slurs, and death threats. People contacted my agent and suggested I should be dropped because of my "anti-white" tendencies. The trolls' responses were always totally disproportionate to the critique—I'd argue it would be pretty cool if police could stop killing unarmed black people, and someone would respond "I hope you become the next hashtag"—but it doesn't matter. Even if you know you're right, eventually you start to get tired.

Social media has always thrived on the kind of drama fueled by callout campaigns—all you have to do is write a single tweet about why what Katy Perry did was #NotOK, and suddenly you've mobilized tens of thousands of people to . . . do what, exactly? The sense of deep moral righteousness each party feels in the heat of the moment, furiously typing out clapbacks and subtweets before members of the opposing #TeamWhoever can get their barbs in, gives the whole thing the illusion of importance when it's almost always infighting, or attention seeking. I used a track-and-field analogy earlier, but sometimes it feels more like the WWE— laying the smack down with the perfect GIF.

After a while, I still felt like I was changing the internet, but I wondered if it might be for the worse. I was letting these attacks consume my time, and more and more it started to feel like my career depended on other people saying stupid shit instead of me saying good shit. I was giving so much of my attention to people who were intentionally posting hateful things online instead of focusing on my own career and my own audience.

It all came to a head in early 2016, around the time I was hired to work on *The Nightly Show with Larry Wilmore*. I was invited to the Sundance Film Festival to participate in a program the festival was cosponsoring with YouTube. It was my first time at

Sundance, and I was excited to attend the premiere of *The Skinny*, a new web series that was going to run on Refinery29. It was being billed as an unapologetically feminist project, and Jill Soloway,* the creator of *Transparent*, was executive-producing it.

So I was pretty surprised when the series began to roll and it was racist. Not, like, a little bit racist, but like *Hot Asian women keep "stealing" men from the white protagonist and it's NOT FAIR* racist. *Black guys are being objectified, but also portrayed as dangerous rapists* racist. *A joke about police brutality in the first episode* racist.

I sat through all six episodes, feeling more and more defeated, and when the lights came on and the panel discussion began, I assumed someone was going to say something. But the praise was rapturous. *The Skinny* was a feminist masterpiece! Its body-positivity was transformative! Jill Soloway and their team were really "standing up to patriarchy"!

When the Q&A period rolled around, I stood up to ask a question. I didn't want to offend Jill, or make a scene—I was invited to Sundance as an up-and-coming voice, I had just gotten my first job writing for TV, and honestly, the altitude was fucking with my head—so I tried to be positive. "There are lot of funny elements in this," I said, "and I want it to succeed. But although Jill mentioned intersectionality, the only women of color in the series were being mocked and resented for their sexuality. The series also fetishized black men while implying that they're dangerous. Why did you go in that direction? Have you considered how to rectify the issue for the next season?"

Jill and the moderator didn't know what to do. Jill went on the defensive; the moderator tried to talk her way out of it. "How are black men being fetishized?" the moderator asked. "It's true! Black men love me, and I'm fat!"

---

* Jill Soloway identifies as genderqueer and nonbinary and prefers to use they/them pronouns.

It was too much. After the panel, I just wanted to get out of there, but as soon as the crowd was dismissed, Jill Soloway and the moderator came over and asked to talk. I didn't really want to, and I told them so, but a crowd was forming, and from a career standpoint, I knew it probably wasn't wise to snub everyone's new favorite television director. But then Jill said something that made me downright sick to my stomach. "You're right," they said. "We need more women of color who write. Where are they?"

For a second, I couldn't say anything. Where are they? I was a black woman who had been invited to Sundance because I was a promising TV writer. I was standing right in front of Jill, and it was like they couldn't see me. Or didn't want to.

I began to feel backed into a corner, literally and figuratively. I heard Jill say, "Next time you're in LA you need to come over." I told them I didn't want to come over and didn't want to be their friend, and that if they wanted more women of color to participate in their projects they would have to work to find them. Maybe start by looking at Sundance? They went back to saying it was actually not racist to produce a scene in which a white woman asks a bunch of black men if they would fuck her and then wonders if black men have lower standards than white guys.

When I finally got back to my hotel room, I was nervous and fuming, and I took out my phone. This is probably not the best way to handle your anger, but it was what I did: I recorded a series of videos, talking about how fucking frustrating the whole thing was, even crying a little at the end, and posted it to my Snapchat.

The video was resonating with other women of color who'd had to deal with white-feminist doublespeak—the "I'm on your side" that becomes "I'm actually more on your side than you are." My fans started encouraging me to post the video on my blog so more people would be able to see it, since Snapchat videos disappear after twenty-four hours. I was still mad, so I slapped on a title—"Here's What Happens When You Call Out White Feminists"—and up it went.

I should have known the post would take off—I was cursing and crying and dropping pop-culture keywords like "Jill Solo-way" and "white feminists." I made it in the heat of the moment and didn't take enough time to process what had happened, which made it ideal content for the internet. Soon enough, blog-gers began to blog, and angry commenters began to harass Jill, leaving comments on their Instagram calling them a racist bitch and saying the world would be better off if they killed themselves. Jill emailed me to let me know they were still on my side, not my enemy, and to again extend the invitation to come to their house. I told them not to email me again.

When the furor died down a few days later, I felt gross on mul-tiple levels. I still had a bad taste in my mouth from the original incident, but I also felt responsible for my fans, who had taken their harassment campaign to inappropriate levels. I worried the frenzy would jeopardize my job on *The Nightly Show*. Even though I'd never directly sic my followers on someone, I was starting to realize how much influence I had. I was not just a girl from South Florida making videos in her bedroom—I had a following of all sorts of random people who could and would do things I don't agree with on my behalf.

There wasn't much I could do at that point—the damage was done. But I was so embarrassed by the hysteria. A couple of weeks later, when Jill announced they would be directing a new Ama-zon series, I saw a comment from someone saying they weren't going to watch the show because of what Jill "did to Franchesca Ramsey." Though it was by no means the strongest language ever used by an internet commenter, it was clear that I'd had a lasting impact on this person's reputation. My story had reached corners of the internet I hadn't anticipated, and I wasn't sure how to feel about it.

I made a vague tweet and Tumblr post reminding my audience that my speaking publicly about an issue or person wasn't a call to arms. From then on, I knew I had to take this stuff more seriously—for my own mental health, for my career, and in order to create the kind of online community I didn't dread participating in.

That's not to say I stopped getting into Twitter arguments, because I didn't. A queen doesn't give up her crown so easily. During my first year on TV, as my visibility increased, I couldn't help but try to defend myself against all the new people, both anonymous and public, coming for me. But I did it the old-fashioned way—passive-aggressive shade. No naming names, and I always shared articles from trusted sources instead of random people whose worldview happened to align perfectly with mine. I realized that if I wanted to effect any actual change, my commentary had to focus on the systems, not individual scapegoats.

I learned the hard way that callout culture is much more complicated than it seems—it's not as simple as "If you see something, say something." I used to treat social media like a tool; in reality, it's more like a double-edged sword. Just as I've developed a career and an audience on YouTube, Facebook, Twitter, Instagram, and Snapchat, I've seen how easy it is for information, whether it's true or false, to spread quickly on these platforms, and I know it's almost impossible to take it back once it's out there. Motives are questionable and drama is real.

Okay, you're probably thinking, *but the internet is full of prejudice and bigotry. What should I do? How do I know if I should call someone out or take the conversation offline? And what am I even supposed to say? You know I'm addicted to Facebook, so don't even think about telling me to delete my account and spend more time with my family.*

I would never tell you to delete your account. (Though you probably should spend more time with your family.) Instead, I made a guide.

CALLING IN VS. CALLING OUT: THE GUIDE

CALL OUT (VERB): TO BRING ATTENTION PUBLICLY TO ANOTHER PERSON'S BIGOTED SPEECH, BEHAVIOR, SOUND BITE, JOKE, LYRIC, ARTICLE, FACEBOOK POST, TWEET, INSTAGRAM STORY, SNAPCHAT STORY, ROLE IN A TELEVISION SHOW OR FILM, OR PERFORMANCE, ESPECIALLY ON *SATURDAY NIGHT LIVE* OR AT THE MTV VIDEO MUSIC AWARDS

GOAL: TO MAKE THE BIGOTED PERSON AWARE OF THEIR MISTAKE AND/OR TO RAISE AWARENESS ABOUT A GIVEN ISSUE

Calling out shady behavior online has become many people's first response when they encounter prejudice, bigotry, or anything they think might possibly indicate prejudice or bigotry if you squint real hard and write a two-thousand-word essay about it. But in most cases, it should be reserved for taking large, powerful entities—celebrities, brands, and media—to task when they screw up. Which they inevitably do. This is because (1) they should know better, and (2) taking Emma "Definitely White" Stone out to coffee to discuss the history of whitewashing in Hollywood wasn't really an option for most of us after she was cast as a mixed-race tour guide in the film *Aloha*. (She was supposed to be a quarter Chinese and a quarter Pacific Islander.) On such a large scale, using social media to criticize the film industry's long tradition of ignoring Asian actresses—and to question white actresses like Emma Stone and Scarlett Johansson for willingly participating in that erasure—is the best and most effective action. These campaigns can snowball into progress; though *Aloha* still came out as planned, both Stone and the director admitted they'd made a mistake, apologized, and said the controversy had opened their eyes. (And the fact that the movie flopped, as did ScarJo's *Ghost in the Shell*, was a healthy serving of poetic justice.) Another example of a successful callout campaign is the #OscarsSoWhite hashtag, created by Twitter user and badass organizer @ReignofApril to highlight the lack of diversity among the 2015 Oscar nominees. After it blew up the following year, the Academy took note and committed to diversifying its membership.

But callouts can happen between two-hundred-follower Joes, too. Say you're wasting your lunch break on Facebook one day when you see that your friend Eric has posted two strongly worded paragraphs dead-naming° the "moronic Trump supporter" Caitlyn Jenner and calling her a "man in a dress." While unfriending Eric is certainly an option, maybe you don't want to unfriend him—last time you two saw each other you had a surprisingly great conversation about buying window blinds. What if he just doesn't know any better? So you decide to call him out and let the rest of your Facebook friends know what will and won't fly on your page.

° *Dead-naming* is using a transgender person's birth name instead of their chosen name.

Attention fam: Since Eric Peterson apparently thinks it's OK to post transphobic garbage about Caitlyn Jenner all over my timeline, I wanted to make something very clear: It's not OK! While I agree that Caitlyn "SUCKS SUCKS SUCKS SUCKS," her bad political opinions have nothing to do with her gender or her body. Please don't make the mistake Eric did and think that just because Caitlyn supports the orange toad in the White House, you can deny her the right to identify however she wants. My feminism extends to women I don't like, however misguided they may be, and so should yours.

On the plus side, you've gotten your point across to more than just "Eric." You might feel pretty good about yourself for standing up for what's right. But by making the conversation public, and tagging Eric in the post, no less, you've also opened the door for drama—not just for the unsuspecting Eric, who may be going through who knows what personal crisis in his own life right now, but also for yourself. It's going to be very hard to resist participating in the ninety-four-comment thread that is about to ensue on your timeline, and your lunch break is almost up. Maybe Eric will see the error of his ways, but I'm willing to bet he'd be more likely to do so if you didn't publicly humiliate him first.

Calling out high-profile brands and celebrities can also backfire. In 2016 the internet was blowing up over a Chinese commercial featuring a "dirty" black man who is transformed into a "clean" Chinese man after a woman forces him into her washing machine. People rightfully deemed the ad "super racist" and "the most racist TV commercial ever made"; think pieces about anti-blackness in media around the world rolled in. But the attention also made the commercial go viral, racking up hundreds of millions of views and, presumably, revenue. While the conversation was necessary, the conspiracy theorist in me often wonders if brands and celebrities are sometimes purposefully "screwing up" in order to ride the viral outrage all the way to the bank. (Before the detergent company apologized and removed the ad from the internet—to the best of their ability—a representative told the *New York Times* they had wanted the commercial to be "sensational.")

Callouts are also risky because you can't unring a bell. If your message is directed at the wrong person—or if any of the details are incorrect—you can end up with a giant mess on your hands. I learned this with the Moskowitz/Cotton Mills fiasco, but it was really driven home to me during one of my (infamous) Twitter rants. A video of an unconscious young girl being sexually assaulted had recently gone viral, and the internet was being predictably awful. My caps lock was unwavering as I batted down trolls left and right. "IF YOU'RE UNCONSCIOUS. YOU! CANNOT! CONSENT! PERIOD! THAT'S RAPE FOLKS!" But streams of nasty comments and memes continued to pour into my mentions as people from all walks of life did Cirque du Soleil-level backflips to explain away this young girl's rape. In my flurry of replies, I noticed one that said something like "Sometimes you get too drunk and stuff happens." After a quick glance at the attached profile, I fired back. "As a woman you should know better. Take your victim-blaming bullshit elsewhere." Instead of replying directly, which would've kept our conversation off my main timeline, I made my reply public so it would be visible to my more than fifty thousand followers and added, "Yet another lost girl upholding the patriarchy. *tear drop emoji*" Soon enough, my followers—as well as random users—started chiming in to say she was a victim blamer and disgrace to women. No girl was safe around her.

But as the girl tried to defend herself it became painfully

obvious that I'd made a terrible mistake. She wasn't victim blaming at all—she was talking about her personal experience. As internet users around the world yelled at her, she tried to explain that she'd been in a similar situation and it wasn't a big deal because ultimately she felt it was her own fault. She wasn't trying to speak for the girl in the video.

I immediately posted a public apology and deleted my original tweet, hoping I could undo some of the damage I'd caused, but it was too late. I sent the girl a private message, asking for forgiveness and trying to reassure her that she'd done nothing to deserve being assaulted. No response. I tried again and got an error message: "This account no longer exists."

I still feel horrible about the way the entire exchange went down. I thought I was doing the right thing, but my quick response was driven by the attention I was getting from my audience. I was being praised for "keeping it real" while disregarding who was on the end of that "realness"—a young girl who needed compassion and support, not a dog pile.

So before you spring into action to take down the latest brand, celebrity, media outlet, or random college student with seventy-eight followers, ask yourself:

1. **What's the issue?** A celebrity denying police brutality in an interview is not the same as a celebrity giving a bad tip at the bar where your friend works.

2. **What's at stake?** Could someone lose friends/their job over this? Or will they just feel really bad (assuming they have a soul and feelings)?

3. **Do I have all the details?** Your bartender friend has always liked to embellish. Is it possible that Olivia Wilde tipped in cash and that's why she wrote "0.00" on the receipt?

4. Why are you doing this? Do you want to raise awareness of a problem, or do you want to raise awareness of your Twitter account, which you believe is scandalously underfollowed?

5. What are the best- and worst-case scenarios following this callout?

6. And finally: Would it be better to *call in* instead?

CALL IN (VERB): TO INITIATE A ONE-ON-ONE CONVERSATION TO MAKE ANOTHER PERSON AWARE OF THEIR OWN BIGOTED SPEECH, BEHAVIOR, ETC.

GOAL: TO HELP AN INDIVIDUAL LEARN FROM THEIR MISTAKE AND MOVE FORWARD PRODUCTIVELY

Whereas callouts can leave you feeling like you successfully rallied a group to save fifty puppies from a burning animal shelter run by Cruella de Vil's competitive stepsister, calling in is more like doing extra-credit homework even though there's a chance it won't improve your grade. When someone you know says something incredibly ignorant, walking them through where they went wrong can be time consuming and emotionally draining. And there's no guarantee it'll even be worth it. Thinking she was just going to have a chill catch-up session with her long-lost college roommate, Problematic Angela could very well get defensive and tell you to get over [insert awful thing she said]. The only thing people hate more than being wrong is admitting they were wrong. Like going to the gynecologist, calling in is awkward at first, but it gets easier every time—though unlike going to the gyno, you will not get a lollipop afterward, or peace of mind about your reproductive health.

The biggest difference between calling out and calling in is tone. While I wouldn't suggest coming out of the gate with social justice lingo, "Hey, asshole! That was transphobic!" feels very different from "Heeeeey... I actually wanted to talk to you about that. It was kind of transphobic." The call-in voice is like the stupid airplane noises you make when you're feeding your nephew a spoonful of veggies. Holding little Brendan's mouth open while you shovel in the mushy peas is not going to make him eat, but the *vroom vroom* sounds make those peas go down easier and might even set him on the path toward healthy eating habits for the future.

Though call-ins work best in person and one-on-one, they can also happen online, and even publicly. When Kerry Washington described Kate Winslet as her "spirit animal" on Twitter, I wasn't the only one who cringed. The term gets thrown around a lot, but most people don't realize it's incredibly disrespectful to Native communities. While plenty of people criticized Kerry's choice of words, I was pleasantly surprised by how many did so by calling her in. Even though it's only 140 characters, @ RanaLaPine's tweet "Please don't use the term 'spirit animal' like that. Disrespectful to indigenous beliefs and communities" strikes the perfect balance: It informs without insulting or putting Kerry on blast. It's straightforward without being too blunt. And while it's no secret that Kerry Washington is the best, I like to believe that the fact that no one called her a shit-stain had something to do with her gracious response: "So, I'd never been schooled to concept that using 'spirit animal' in the way I just did is cultural appropriation. I get it. I apologize. TY!" What did we do to deserve someone so heavenly?

After I became disillusioned with my role as YouTube's callout queen, I began toying with the idea of a softer approach. Soon, I had an opportunity to test it out at a tech conference when a woman came out of nowhere and uttered the five words every natural-haired girl dreads (no pun intended): "Can I touch your hair?"

The woman asking already had her hand outstretched, inches away from my perfectly coiled locs. We were all scarfing hors d'oeuvres, so when I think of this memory I always imagine her fingers covered in grease. I swerved out of the way just in time and tried to smile as I responded, "I'd rather you not."

Who knows why, but homegirl was not having it. You'd think I'd just spit in her tuna tartare and asked her to thank me. "Are you serious?" she asked. "Why? Seriously, why not? You can touch my hair." Her voice trembled as she repositioned herself, planted her feet, and leaned her head toward me, as if most people walk around just desperate to tousle strangers' updos. In that moment I knew she wished she could ask to speak to the manager.

"Lemme ask you something," she continued. "Do you always wear your hair that way?" Was she trying to trick me? I hesitated for a second and then said no, I didn't normally wear my hair in curls. "Right," she responded, seeming satisfied. "So then you have to expect that people will want to touch your hair if it doesn't always look like that."

It made no sense. But instead of telling her she was being ridiculous and low-key racist, I decided to take the high road. "Look," I said. "There's a long history of black women's bodies and hair being constantly poked, prodded, and disrespected, so it's really not the same when you offer to let me touch your hair in exchange. I'm sure you didn't mean any harm, but I'm not a petting zoo."

The woman looked at me with a mix of confusion, embarrassment, and guilt, similar to the way my dog Filthy looks when I catch him pulling a pair of underwear out of my hamper. "Here, let's start over," I added, feeling—I'll be honest—pretty smug. "Hi, I'm Franchesca." She timidly shook my hand and introduced herself.

I can't tell you what her name was, because by that point I'd moved on to my victory lap. I pretended like nothing had happened and introduced myself to the small group of eavesdroppers who had gathered around us. While I can't say for sure whether the woman learned something that day, on a personal level, I felt much better than I did after spending six hours in a Twitter-induced rage.

Calling in is generous, because it shows you're not giving up on someone, but it can also be an act of self-care: You're saving yourself the emotional energy that comes with giving in to anger. I could've easily gotten angry with that woman at the party, and I'd have had every right to: She had been disrespectful at best and racist at worst. But I knew that calling her out and drawing attention to her racism would have done both of us more harm than good. I would have spent the rest of the conference feeling upset and guilty, and no one wants to network with someone who's distracted and angry. Plus, making a scene would have made me look really bad.

So: Let's say you want to call in your childhood best friend or cousin. How do you start? Let's go back to the Caitlyn Jenner rant, but now, instead of Eric Peterson, the random guy who convinced you to spring for the full blackout shades in your bedroom, the transphobic garbage is coming from your partner, your favorite uncle, or a close friend. Suddenly, cutting ties isn't a viable option.

An effective call-in is honest, informative, cautionary, and direct: HICD. Hic'd? Sorry there isn't a better acronym; believe me, I tried. You can remember this because...there will most likely be *hiccups* throughout this difficult chat?

Here's how it should go:

Honest: There's no reason to dance around the subject, so let the person know what you want to talk about up front, and then clearly state how their comment made you feel. The goal is to drive home that this conversation is important to you and your relationship.

"Hey, Jude. Can we talk about that Caitlyn Jenner comment you made the other day? It made me uncomfortable, and I want us to get on the same page about it."

Informative: Next, go over exactly what happened as you saw it, and then dig into why the comment or behavior was hurtful. You don't need to go full TED Talk here—you don't want this to feel like a lecture—but if you've got personal anecdotes or historical context to strengthen your explanation, that could really help. It's also important to link the behavior to the broader societal issue that it reinforces—it's not just about personal hurt feelings, but about supporting a culture of oppression and mistreatment.

"Look, there are plenty of things to criticize Caitlyn for. She's oblivious to her white privilege and her class privilege, and she uses her power as a celebrity recklessly. But her being trans has nothing to do with those privileges; her gender identity is separate from the fact that she is not very smart and voted for Cheetolini. Referring to her by her old name and gender is not only disrespectful to her—it says to all trans people that their experiences can be invalidated as soon as they do something wrong."

Cautionary: At this point in the conversation, most people get defensive and try to steer you over the "That's not what I meant" bridge or the "It wasn't my intention to offend you" path. I told you this wouldn't be easy. Thankfully, that rickety bridge and dusty road both lead directly to the "Intent doesn't absolve impact" bush. That one's pretty thorny to wriggle out of. Help them out gently.

> "I know it's hard to stand up for people who are shitty; I don't want to excuse the ignorant things Caitlyn has said and done. <u>But bigotry is not a shortcut to criticism."</u>

While the "It wasn't my intention" nonapology often gets conversations off track, it can be worth indulging—but only just a little. Drive home that intention doesn't take back the damage done, and make it clear that if they don't want to be misunderstood or misrepresented, they need to be more cautious.

> "I'm sure you didn't mean it like that, but saying that sort of thing makes you sound transphobic. And I know that's not you."

When people are inevitably hung up on their intentions, I once heard this analogy: If you accidentally step on someone's toe and break it, it doesn't matter that you didn't mean to break their toe. The toe is still broken, and you have to make up for that somehow.

Direct: The entire conversation should be direct, but if they're feeling confused or mad or like the whole world is shifting around them, you can also steer them to some resources in case they want to learn more. If they seem receptive, send links to videos, articles, or other media that can offer additional perspective.

~~~~~~~~~~

Now it's time for some cold, hard truth. As admirable as calling in may be, sometimes...it doesn't work. It takes a certain level of empathy, maturity, and introspection to make it through these kinds of conversations, and not everyone is cut out for it. For some people, acknowledging their privilege and recognizing how their words or actions uphold oppression is too big of an ask. While I believe that anyone can grow and learn, I know that not everyone wants to. "I'm sorry you feel that way" will always be easier to say than "I'm sorry I made you feel that way. I'll do better."

Even more cold, hard truth: Whether you're calling someone out or in, your relationship to the person matters, both in how you decide how to act (are they worth the trouble?) and in how they'll take your message. Remember the white guy who made that video explaining why "Shit White Girls Say to Black Girls" wasn't racist? A lot of people were (rightfully) mad about the implications of that post—the idea that no one will listen when black people tell their own stories, so white people have to speak for them.

Unfortunately, that white guy was actually onto something. It's scientifically proven that people are more receptive to criticism when it comes from someone who looks like them. In 2016, Kevin Munger, a researcher at the NYU Social Media and Political Participation lab, decided he wanted to see if it was even possible to limit racist harassment on social media. Though they're getting better, social platforms themselves are really bad at stopping their users from spewing hot, bigoted bile into the world—research shows that although banning users who harass other users works in the short term, in the long run it can actually fuel whatever behavior it attempted to curb. Getting punished— whether by being called out or banned—makes harassers feel victimized when they encounter the consequences of their own behavior. Some might call this kind of oversensitivity "being a snowflake," but that would be petty and we don't want to do that. Armed with the understanding that punishment from "the man" had the potential to backfire, Munger wondered whether regular people might do a better job at fighting racist trolls.

So, as one does, he built some fake Twitter accounts. (He called them "bots" even though he controlled them.) One group of bots had a white guy in their profile pictures (and names like Greg), and the other group had a black person in their profile pictures (and names like Rasheed). Sounds plausible, right? Munger gave the bots varying numbers of followers, from a handful to around five hundred, suspecting that "high status" users who had more followers would be more persuasive than some guy named Steve with eleven friends.

Armed with these catfish bros, Munger began to search particular racial slurs on Twitter. Switching off between Gregs and Rasheeds, he responded to users who had a history of racist harassment with the same message:

> @[racist person] Hey man, just remember that there are real people who are hurt when you harass them with that kind of language

Munger chose to respond to users who presented as white men on Twitter or were completely anonymous. Then, he tracked their tweets for two months after he responded to them, to see whether they kept tweeting racist bullshit or reformed and turned into Maxine Waters fan accounts.

The results were surprising, but also not surprising. The only group that was able to significantly reduce the racists' use of slurs was—can you guess?—the white guys with five hundred followers. Obviously, this suggests that if you want a white guy to see the error in his racism, you should have a white guy point it out to him.

But it got more depressing: Turns out, when white guys are called out by black guys, it can actually make them *more* racist. In certain cases, Munger found that Rasheed just made things worse, with users increasing their usage of slurs in the months following the reply. Unfortunately, "sanctioning behaviors" that highlight the difference between the two parties involved don't usually work. (Munger's research is published in the journal *Political Behavior*, if you want to check it out in full.)

This principle—that people in a given community have to be accountable for educating others in that community—doesn't just apply to conversations about racism. Cis people need to step up and talk to other cis people about their casual transphobia, dude bros should talk to other dude bros about the importance of consent, and so on. And while there are no guarantees, finding common ground can often make things easier. When Jenna Marbles emailed me to apologize for the "Things I Don't Understand" video, I responded. But I didn't want to gloat or insult her, or overwhelm her with a rant about how her apology would never be able to erase the psychological damage she'd inflicted on innocent teenagers. I don't think that's true, and I don't think she's a bad person. However, I did encourage her to admit her mistake and apologize publicly. Her platform had only grown since the incident, and sexual assault within the YouTube community is becoming more and more of a visible problem. People are so bad at apologizing and taking responsibility for their mistakes, I wrote, that if she did it, so many people who look up to her might learn something.

As far as I know, she still hasn't come out about the incident. But sometimes people surprise you. A year after my Sundance back-and-forth with Jill Soloway, the *Los Angeles Times* reported on a similar argument that broke out over a women-in-film lunch at the very same festival. Guests like Shirley MacLaine and Salma Hayek were discussing the recent election of Donald Trump and the importance of not feeling "victimized" when Jessica Williams, *The Daily Show*'s former "senior Beyoncé correspondent" and all-around black Renaissance woman, started to speak.

"What if you are a person of color, or a transgendered [sic] person who—just from how you look—you already are in a conflict?" she asked the table.

The conversation began to get heated, and some of the guests, especially Salma Hayek, began objecting to Jessica's tone, or even to the idea that she should identify as a black woman at all. Ah, yes, the old notion that "not seeing race" makes racism go away. People were speaking over her. The conversation was beginning to slip away. And then Jill Soloway stepped in.

"With intersectional feminism, it's our responsibility as white women to recognize that when there are people of color or people who are queer—we need to prioritize your voices and let you speak the loudest and learn from your experience, because we haven't been listening," Jill said to the table. "So please, Jessica, finish your thoughts."

When I read this story, my eyes were so wide I'm surprised they didn't fall out of my head. Jill had nailed it. Not only did they school the women at the table, they passed the mic back to Jessica like a seasoned backup singer assisting with the chorus before falling back for the next verse. Despite the tears, heated emails, and nasty Instagram comments of the previous year, I couldn't help but wonder: Had I, in some small way, helped Jill become the ally they were that day?

If there were some foolproof way to mend hearts and relationships when these kinds of awkward situations arise, you best believe I wouldn't put it in a book—I'd patent it, sell it on QVC for four easy payments of $19.95, and put the rest of my lineage through college. But my kids will probably end up taking out loans like everyone else, because there is no magic solution for opening, or changing, people's minds. There will undoubtedly be times where there's no resolution, and you'll leave the conflict frustrated and drained. And then there will be other times, maybe a month or even a few years later, when it will all feel worth it.

CHAPTER FOUR

BETWEEN A LOC AND A HARD PLACE

The Chescalocs Story

The only thing worse than asking to touch a black woman's hair is "asking" while simultaneously stroking her luscious curls as if you were at a petting zoo. And while this is a particularly common experience for black women, in reality it often feels as if black and brown folks with any sort of kink or curl are forced to move through the world like they're guarding classified government files on their heads. Thankfully the politics surrounding black hair have become much more visible over the last few years. More people are accepting their natural textures and are less hesitant to lay the smack down when people start policing, ogling, fondling, yanking, and making rude comments about the "omg so weird!" texture of black hair.

These days, there's a booming natural hair community online, which has led more people to feel like "going natural" is a viable option—politically, practically, and professionally. YouTube is filled with hair tutorials, product demos, and Q&A videos for every black hair texture and style imaginable. There are hundreds of forums and sites where women exchange salon recommendations and offer support to those tinkering with the idea of transitioning their hair. And it's not just on YouTube: In 2016, my friend Phoebe Robinson published an essay collection called *You Can't Touch My Hair: And Other Things I Still Have to Explain*; the same year, Solange released the track "Don't Touch My Hair."

In retrospect, going natural was the jumping-off point for my career as an activist and as an online performer. When I decided to go natural in 2003, the year after I graduated high school, conversations around natural hair were almost nonexistent in my world. There was no "ethnic" hair section in my local drugstore, and when I went looking for guidance for styling and maintaining my locs I quickly learned there wasn't much in the way of support. Little did I know the decision to start making hairstyle videos of my own would be the gateway to conversations about race and identity, along with the start of an amazing community and career.

I've often found that nonblack people are perplexed by the ongoing conversations around black hair and the importance of going natural in our community. As many black thinkers and writers have pointed out, for us it's never "just hair," but a symbol of hundreds of years of oppression and struggle. Throughout history, black people have been told their natural hair texture is unacceptable, dirty, and unprofessional. And while there's nothing inherently bad about the desire to straighten one's natural hair, resisting the subtle and sometimes overt messages in media that equate straight hair with success isn't always easy. Not to mention, going natural as an adult after rocking a perm for years is scary as hell. It's essentially like learning a language you spoke in childhood but haven't heard in over a decade. And then when you go natural, you're expected to be fluent in that language to get ready every morning.

As a kid, I begged my mother to let me relax my hair. In retrospect, I had no idea what I was asking for, nor did I grasp how backward it was to call chemically straightening one's hair "relaxing"—as if Afro-textured hair needs to be tamed and calmed with chemicals. I've often joked that *The Relaxer* sounds like a crappy horror movie in which a maniacal killer tortures natural-haired women with scorching-hot chemical ooze and then forces them to pay him money for it.

While my mother had worn her hair long and straight for as long as I could remember, she was determined to make me wait until I was "old enough" to handle the responsibilities of maintaining my hair: biweekly deep-conditioning treatments, learning how to wrap my hair at night to help cut down on styling time in the morning, avoiding excessive heat, and of course rocking a swim cap at the pool. (The last thing you want to do is mix chlorine with your relaxed hair.) Remind me again why this process is called a "relaxer" when it takes so much work to maintain? When do I get to chill and not think about what's happening on my head?

Although I was one of only a small handful of black students at my predominantly white Catholic elementary school, and part of an even smaller group of girls with natural hair, I didn't feel the pressure to straighten my hair at school. Instead, it was my relatives who treated chemical straightening as if it were inevitable, or required. When I'd visit my family in South Carolina, they would say things like "When is your mother going to do something with that hair?" Which really just means "When are you finally getting a relaxer?" One year, I got braids before heading to South Carolina for the summer, and my aunt promptly took them out and used a hot comb to straighten my hair. She knew better than to give me a relaxer without my mother's permission, but my mom was still livid. Not because my hair was straight, but because she had spent "good money" on the braids and they were cute as hell.

When my mother finally gave in and let me relax my hair in fourth grade, the reality of my decision quickly set in. Sure, my hair was now shiny, silky, and straight, but it felt like it never grew—it was always so damaged that I had to constantly trim and cut it off to keep it looking "healthy." The chemicals were clearly too strong for my hair, and I was constantly shedding, so much that my stylist gave me an asymmetrical haircut to mask the damage. Thankfully my sideways mullet (short on the right and long on the left) was reminiscent of Salt-N-Pepa, who I later learned also rocked the style after singeing the hell out of their hair back in the day.

When I think back to the years I wore my hair bone straight, I can't remember white people asking to touch it or fondling my head without permission. There's a sad irony in the fact that white people never tried to touch my hair until I went natural—that I had to do something totally unnatural to my head in order to blend in, because my hair in its most natural state was deemed weird or different.

In my freshman year of high school, my super-cool and super-rebellious best friend Melissa convinced me to add highlights to my hair using an at-home dye kit. While I'd never dyed my hair before, Melissa (who was white) was an old pro. Only neither of us knew that the process wouldn't be so easy for me. I opted for a dark maroon, hoping a few streaks to my bangs would be subtle enough to be cool and to hide from my mom. The result was far from subtle.

At first, the streaks were barely visible. I hadn't realized that you need to bleach dark hair in order for any color to show up on it. Though I was disappointed, I found solace in the fact that I wouldn't have to deal with the possibility of my mother flipping out over my new highlights. But my punishment ended up being way worse. The next time I got my hair done, I didn't tell my stylist I'd colored my hair—I didn't think there was a point, since you couldn't even see it. As she washed out the relaxer, she also washed away half my bangs. My hair began falling out in huge clumps, and I had only myself and a box of Clairol to blame.

I was devastated, but I wasn't about to ditch my relaxer. Instead I spent the rest of high school with awful haircuts that tried and failed to hide my temples, where my hairline was patchy and uneven. You know those videos of the toddlers who cut their own hair when their parents leave the room? It looked kind of like that—I'm sure a few people wondered who had left me alone with the grown-up scissors.

My love of bangs grew deeper as I figured they were the only things standing between me and total mortification. Little by little, the starting point of my bangs inched farther and farther back, toward the crown of my head, so they would cover my forehead as evenly as possible. When my bangs no longer cut it, I'd fill in my hairline with mascara, and if I ever got caught in the rain I'd make a mad dash, cupping my foam bra inserts in one hand and covering my edges with the other to keep Maybelline Great Lash from streaming down my face.

Despite my hair woes, I took comfort in the beautiful images of black women, natural or not, in the pages of my mom's issues of *Essence*, *Ebony*, and *Jet*. I LIVED for *Jet*'s Beauty of the Week feature, where the magazine would highlight an absolutely stunning black woman—usually wearing a bikini and posed next to a waterfall, beach, or community pool—who read the magazine. The girls were always very fit (which was intimidating), but they wore lots of different hairstyles, which I loved.

All the other magazines I read back then were dominated by white girls; any time I saw a black girl grace their pages it was like a brief portal into another reality. *Sassy* was very feminist and progressive, but I wouldn't describe it as diverse. I liked that the models weren't super skinny, but I can't say I remember seeing anyone that looked like me. When *Sassy* went out of print, I graduated to *Jane*, which I loved for how snarky and raw it felt. I had no idea if it was accurate, since I'd never had sex, but *Jane* writers really seemed like they were being honest and real about sex. (I can't say when the It Happened to Me column jumped the shark—I know it was long before that notorious viral article "My Gynecologist

Found a Ball of Cat Hair in My Vagina"—but I loved to read it growing up. No shame.) I thought *Jane*'s street-style pieces, which featured women of all different races and sizes, were so cool, and I got a lot of ideas from them. *NYLON* was the opposite of relatable, but I loved the music features and magazine's design; I'd make poor copies of their illustrations in my sketchbook and tell myself that if I couldn't be a singer or an actress, maybe I could move to New York and work for *NYLON* someday.

When I left South Florida for my brief stint at acting school in Michigan, I struggled to take care of my hair. The nearest black salon was over an hour away, I had no car and limited funds, and the first few weeks of freshman year were doing a number on my already crunchy hair. The cool fall climate and drunken nights when I'd forget to wrap my hair didn't help. I decided to take the plunge and grow it out in hopes of going natural. A girl in my dorm agreed to braid my hair in exchange for twenty-five dollars and a few swipes on my meal card. And with that my journey was under way.

After rocking cornrows and micro braids all year, I needed to figure out who I wanted to be when I was ready to set my natural hair free. So I decided to be Lauryn Hill. Like the rest of the world, I'd been obsessed with her debut album, *The Miseducation of Lauryn Hill*, and I loved everything about her, especially her hair. Besides Whoopi Goldberg, she was the only celebrity I'd seen wearing locs, so I scoured the internet for pictures of her hair at every stage, hoping to get an idea of what I might look like. Maybe some part of me thought that if I had locs I would look like Lauryn. (Spoiler: Didn't happen.) But I also loved how Afrocentric, unique, and, most of all, confident her hair made her look. She was everything I wanted to be.

Today my locs are nearing fifteen years old and hang just below my waist. I love piling them on top of my head into a giant messy bun mountain, wrapping them with bright colorful scarves, and braiding and pinning them into twisting and turning sculptures that resemble the fancy garden trees from *Alice in Wonderland*. I wear all 114 of my locs (yes, I've counted—partially out of curiosity and partially because people kept asking how many I have) proudly.

But the journey from baby locs to black Rapunzel was a long and frustrating one. The summer after my freshman year of college, I decided to finally do the big chop, trimming off my relaxed ends to rock a teeny-weeny Afro (TWA). I assigned my mom the task of cutting my hair. While I was nervous to take the leap, my mom was even more so. "Franchesca, there isn't much hair here," she kept saying, in Worried Mom voice. "It's gonna be short. Are you sure?"

I was sure. I don't think my mother disliked my TWA, per se (I'm basically a rapper now), but she worried I hadn't really considered how difficult it might be to adjust to my natural-hair texture as an adult. She also remembered the countless nights I'd cried over my broken hair, lopsided boobs, giant feet, and admittedly horselike, gummy smile. She was probably worried that cutting my hair would send me into another puddle of tears, and that this time it would be her fault. But to both her surprise and mine, I loved my tiny fro and wore Bantu knots and twist-outs all summer long.

A year later, my mom's friend Yevola, who'd had locs for more than fifteen years, started my baby locs for me when I moved back to Florida to go to school in Miami. She told me to retwist my hair every few weeks, showed me how to do it, gave me a jar of her favorite gel, and sent me on my way. After that, I was on my own.

Baby locs are often referred to as being in the "ugly stage," because they're short and you can't do much with them, which is...similar to a baby in many ways. But I never thought of them that way—babies aren't ugly, they're cute. Sure, they try your patience, but you're made better for it. Or so I've heard.

There wasn't a lot of information available on how to style locs online, and you certainly couldn't buy natural-hair products at Walgreens, so I was stuck trying to figure out my hair on my own, on top of being at a new school in a new city. There were a lot of black-hair supply stores in Miami, but I had no clue what products to use, and I didn't really love my mom's friend's favorite gel, so I started buying random things and seeing what I liked.

Much like a baby, I wore lots of hats and scarves at first. My mom would occasionally send me scarves she'd found at discount stores or consignment shops, which was sweet, though she'd also ask if I had anything to add "shine" to my locs, which isn't a thing. (Sorry, Mom.) My extended family gave me a harder time. My uncle asked why I'd cut my hair off; I'd had "such pretty hair." My aunts would say things like "You're brave to go natural—I don't think I could do it." And despite her being natural the entire time I've been on this earth, my grandmother still occasionally asks, "Is that all yours, Frannie?" even though I've told her a dozen times, "Yes, this is my hair, Grandma, and please don't call me Frannie."

Faced with these well-meaning but limited resources, I joined the only online dreadlock° community I could find: LiveJournal's Get Up Dread Up forum. If you Google this group today, you will notice that it is basically the same as it was in 2004: almost entirely made up of white people. (Shout out to Danielle Henderson, a badass writer and one of the only other black people on the site.) Most GUDU members were friendly, but one of the moderators and I butted heads a lot. She regularly discouraged me from twisting my hair or using product, which really pissed me off. I was far from an expert—that's why I'd joined this ragtag group of hacky sack bongo players in the first place—but she wouldn't admit that

---

° You'll notice I usually call my hair "locs" and not "dreadlocks." There's nothing dreadful about my hair.

her hair was just fundamentally different from mine and required different care.

After lurking around GUDU for a few months, watching my hair grow and change and becoming increasingly frustrated with the lack of content geared toward black hair, I decided to make my first tutorial, which became my first YouTube video. Although I was still learning about my hair through trial and error, I knew there had to be other people who could benefit from my experiences.

For a while, I posted my hair tutorials alongside my music and comedy videos on the same channel, Chescaleigh, but as the demand for natural hair content grew (like my hair...sorry), I eventually started a dedicated hair channel, Chescalocs. Since there was no formula for beauty videos then like there is today, I got creative: I did updos inspired by Tilda Swinton in *The Chronicles of Narnia*, Janelle Monáe, the bow Lady Gaga wore in the "Poker Face" era, and Medusa. (The last one was for Halloween, but if you want to embody a powerful female monster from Greek mythology in your day-to-day, power to you.) I dispelled common misconceptions about locs (they're not dirty!), did product reviews, shared maintenance tips, and tried to convey what, to me, is one of the most beautiful aspects of black hair: You can sculpt it into a piece of art. As I forced myself to come up with new ideas for videos for my growing audience—I was kind of hard on myself about posting regularly—I got more and more excited about the natural hair movement that was developing around me. I was encouraging people to start their own locs as I challenged preconceptions about black hair. Our hair isn't smelly or unruly. It's regal—it's the only texture on earth that extends to the sun like a crown!

When *Paper* magazine selected me for its annual Beautiful People list in 2012, I realized how my newfound activism and my long-running love of beauty could intersect. There I was, locs and all, alongside up-and-coming celebrities like David Oyelowo, Zosia Mamet, Rita Ora, John Mulaney, and Rebel Wilson. It was so surreal. Although I'd been publishing a beauty vlog for years, I never would have described myself as "beautiful" before. Cute? Sure. Attractive? Mildly. But not *beautiful*. It was my first professional photo shoot, and since I'd always felt really insecure about my looks, especially my body, I went into it worried about what they'd make me wear. (It ended up being a strapless Kenzo dress, which was cute but not exactly appropriate for the freezing January rain out there on the balcony. Especially when you consider that I wasn't wearing a bra.) I spent the whole shoot questioning the stylists' and photographer's choices: Bright magenta lipstick? But I never wore lip color! "Sexy" smoldering eye? But I'd rather smile! I was so trapped inside my own head at the time that I was shocked when I saw the feature in print: I looked awesome. Not only was I side by side with some gorgeous and talented people, but I kinda seemed like I belonged there.

In many ways, the *Paper* shoot showed me what I'd been saying all along with my channel: Whether I knew it or not, Chescalocs had always been about embracing and celebrating black beauty in a world that, historically, has always said blackness is less desirable. One of the reasons I know my trolls are a waste of time: Whenever they discover my hair tutorials, they're confused—they still hate me, but they don't see anything to be righteously angry about in those videos. They don't understand that my hair is just as much an expression of blackness as my social justice work.

Although I haven't made hair videos in years—they can take hours to film—I still get tons of messages from people around the world saying that I inspired them to start locs, or taught them how to style their hair. When I had the chance to meet Oscar-nominated and Emmy Award–winning director Ava DuVernay at a charity event a few years ago, I almost had a heart attack when she told me she'd watched my videos for styling tips. And while it's incredible to learn that celebs like Ava have enjoyed my videos, it's especially gratifying to now see young girls unapologetically wearing locs, and to see young loc'd celebrities like Willow Smith and Chloe x Halle that kids can look up to.

The proudest moment of my career came a few years ago, when I had the opportunity to meet Tiana Parker, a third grader who was sent home from her Oklahoma charter school in 2013 for wearing her hair in locs. Shortly after her story went viral, her parents contacted me on Facebook and shared that Tiana was a fan of my videos and had decided to loc her hair after seeing my tutorials. They were coming to New York for a long weekend and hoped I could make time to meet Tiana and possibly offer some words of encouragement. To know that a little girl found the confidence to love and embrace her natural hair because of me—even as her own school had the nerve to tell her it was "distracting" and not "presentable"—in some small way helped me get over the absolute rage I felt about this school's racist policy. (Afros and Mohawks were also forbidden.)

I wish this were a shocking anecdote, but policing black hair in this way is disturbingly common. In 2017, two sixteen-year-old twin sisters at a charter school in Massachusetts were told their braided hair extensions were "distracting" and in violation of the dress code. When they refused to "fix" their hair, they were banned from extracurriculars and prom and threatened with suspension. In 2016, Durham's School for Creative Studies made a group of students remove the head wraps they were wearing to celebrate Black History Month. In 2013, a private school in Orlando threatened to expel twelve-year-old Vanessa VanDyke, whose voluminous natural look was so fierce that I'm kind of questioning my locs right now, if she didn't cut or shape her hair. Earlier that year, a twenty-four-year-old secretary in Saint Louis was forced to choose between her job and the locs she'd been growing out for ten years. In 2012, a meteorologist was fired from her local TV news station for defending her TWA against racist Facebook commenters. In 2014, the U.S. Army caused an uproar by briefly considering a ban on "twists, dreadlocks, Afros, and braids" for female soldiers, and servicewomen were permitted to wear dreadlocks and twists only in January 2017, after many had spent years getting relaxers despite the damage, cost, and danger. (After the restriction was lifted, Major Tennille Woods Scott told *Vogue* that she used to relax her own hair while stationed in Iraq in 2007 and 2008. "In the hour or so that it took," she said, "I was nervous, thinking, *What if a rocket or mortar comes in?*") Meanwhile, with the support of her parents, Tiana Parker ended up transferring schools so she could keep wearing her hair the way she wanted to.

I once saw a quote that said, "Be who you needed when you were younger." This simple yet powerful sentence has since informed my work across comedy, social justice, and beauty. When I was Tiana's age, I was begging my mother to straighten my hair—I didn't find the confidence to go natural until my early twenties. I can't imagine having that level of confidence and self-knowledge at just seven years old. While I wish it hadn't taken me so long to arrive at a place where I truly love myself, I now realize the process of going natural and learning how to style and take care of my hair on my own is tied up with my journey into adulthood and self-acceptance.

As my platform grows, I see how important it is for people to see a black woman wearing her natural hair proudly. I'm now becoming the woman I needed to see in media when I was Tiana's age, and that's pretty powerful stuff. The online beauty community has changed a lot since I was explaining how I put my hair in a ponytail in a dimly lit hair tutorial in 2006. What used to feel free and open—a community for everyone—has since been tainted by the growing desire to be famous and make money.

Although Photoshop has long been a strategy of fashion magazines and ad campaigns—when I briefly worked at Maybelline, I had the job of making the models' eyelashes even thicker and longer for mascara ads—now everyone on social media or YouTube has the tools to alter themselves to blemish-free perfection. And the way brands have jumped on the opportunity to shape "influencers" has totally warped what "beautiful" means to many people. From waist trainers to hair gummies and flat-tummy tea, social media is filled with people pushing shady brands in exchange for a check, and their fans are none the wiser. "USE MY PRODUCT CODE" should be a warning that a supposedly "real" beauty blogger is being paid to recommend a certain product or service—but so many girls and women fall for it anyway.

It's hard to be part of an industry that you realize is so damaging. But that's also part of why I continue to be vocal and visible about what goes into my style, and about when and if I choose to work with brands, even if I'm no longer making step-by-step tutorials every week. I know it's possible to be the change you want to see in your community and if my story helps just one person start down the path to loving who they are, all the better.

CHAPTER FIVE

LESSONS FROM GOING PUBLIC, PART 1

If You Can't Stand the Heat, Get Out of the Spotlight

The first time I felt the tingle of celebrity potential was in college, when I wrote and recorded an original song that was selected for the *Jane* magazine reader CD. Along with its snarky takes on sex, relationships, pop culture, and fashion, *Jane* would periodically send out mix CDs with the magazine. When the editors announced a special edition featuring reader-submitted jams, I saw my chance. I'd spent the entire summer working on a few songs with the huge loser I was sort of dating who liked to cut demos in his dad's home studio, and I submitted one of them to *Jane*'s contest. When my funky, wannabe–Ani DiFranco ditty "I Know How the Story Goes" was selected for the album, Columbia Records sent me a letter saying I had "promise." All I'd have to do was shell out for a real demo and make something a little "more commercial." I knew at that moment I was on the brink of stardom.

Of course, I wasn't. I lost access to the recording studio when loser-guy-I-wasn't-even-dating dumped me—it was for the best, trust me—and it would be years before I gained a fraction of the recognition I thought my little achievement was 100 percent definitely about to usher in.

I wish I could say the disappointment taught me not to count my Golden Globes before they hatch, but unfortunately this kind of wishful thinking became a pattern. A few years later, in 2008, I was living in Miami when I entered YouTube's RedCarpet Reporter contest on a whim. Although my entry was poorly lit, and I stumbled over my words more than a few times, apparently the judges were taken with my skills as I interviewed Pat and our dog Filthy for the imaginary Golden Pooch Awards; I made it to the second round. But this proved harder than I anticipated—the contest was then opened up to a public vote. I busted my ass to promote my entry, sending out a press release to local newspapers and even throwing a party, complete with laptop-voting stations. My hustling paid off, and I was awarded the chance to report from the Emmys red carpet on behalf of YouTube and People.com. After an incredible weekend in LA, dancing with Niecy Nash, cracking jokes with Kathy Griffin, and singing on the red carpet with Josh Groban, I was certain I'd snag a job with *People* and be forced to give my two weeks' notice to the Miami Beach Chamber of Commerce, where I worked as the communications manager.

Sadly, I left with a "don't call us, we'll call you" before flying back to Florida and heading straight to the office. I was so devastated by my return to normal life that I gave away my giant bag of Emmy swag (filled with jewelry, makeup, gourmet snacks, and tech goodies) to my coworkers and pouted at my desk.

In 2011, I entered YouTube's NextUp contest, which promised to find YouTube's next big stars and give them the training and tools to hit it big. Once again I scrambled to submit an entry and get my friends and family to vote for me; I was selected as one of thirty-five creators to receive a hefty check and a week's worth of video production training at the Google offices. I spent the week listening to lectures from giant YouTubers like the Gregory Brothers and Michelle Phan and former executives from Nickelodeon and MTV. I hung on every word and took meticulous notes. YouTube believed I had what it took to become a star, and I was determined to prove them right.

The following year, "SWGSTBG" went viral, and once again, I was sure my big break had arrived. It was obvious that the video was a major turning point in my career, but again, it wasn't exactly the launch into stardom that I thought it would be. That's the thing about turning points: Facing a new direction doesn't mean there's not another long road in front of you.

The "SWGSTBG" numbers seemed like undeniable proof that I would be picking out Emmy dresses in no time. But after I quit my job, signed with my agent, and informed my friends and family that they could expect *much* better Christmas presents in the coming years—I planned on being very generous as a wealthy celebrity—I didn't get any work. I went on audition after audition, but never booked anything bigger than a failed Oxygen pilot and a role as a sexy coworker in a Wendy's radio commercial I still haven't heard. I maintained my rigorous twice-a-week YouTube posting schedule, but the viral gods had moved on to Donna the Deer Lady and the German guy who did a cannonball onto a pool of ice. After about a year, I got a manager, and together we developed a show called *The Franchesca Feed*, which would have been a sketch comedy show organized like an endlessly scrolling Facebook feed. We pitched it to twelve networks—everyone from Bravo to Lifetime to MTV. No one wanted it.

In retrospect I'm glad this didn't work out, because an endlessly scrolling Facebook feed is my worst nightmare. It was also clear that I wasn't ready for my own show. Nevertheless, my YouTube money was seriously dwindling, so I took a job blogging about social justice at Upworthy, a viral content site known for popularizing the "You Won't Believe What Happened Next" style of headline. Working there would teach me a lot about how to engage—or, okay, sometimes trick—an audience online. And since I worked from home, I was able to enjoy the benefits of a regular check and health insurance and still squeeze in auditions and speaking engagements in my spare time.

Although we didn't get a single offer to produce *The Franchesca Feed*, MTV said they liked me and wanted to keep in touch. After I went on another series of failed auditions for shows like *Hey Girl* (originally known as *Blogger Girls*) and *Girl Code*, in 2014 they asked if I'd be interested in developing a web series. They'd had success with *Braless*, which broke down feminist concepts in a fun, straightforward way by relating them to pop culture and current events, and they wondered if I could do a similar series about race. They hooked me up with the Kornhaber Brown production company (who also produced *Braless*), and together we began to develop what would, in over a year, become *Decoded*.

From the get-go, it was exhausting to toggle back and forth between the production company, Upworthy, auditions, and any other gigs my agent snagged for me. But having my own show had always been my dream, and although *Decoded* wasn't going to be on network television, it was one step closer to network television, so I did whatever I could to make it work. I would fly across the country for a college speaking gig, write Upworthy posts from my hotel room after my speech, spend the plane ride home researching and writing stories, and, between remote company meetings, run to my producer's offices to hammer out topics for *Decoded*. After two months, we had a pitch for MTV. They were into it—but little did I know, we weren't anywhere close to being done. We spent another four months negotiating contracts, and another couple more ironing out the concept, fighting about the name (it was not always *Decoded*), building a new set (we hated the first one), and shooting and reshooting (I had no idea how to do my own makeup).

The entire time I was working on this, people would ask me what the hell had happened to me. Though I'm not ashamed to do a little self-promotion, I started to dread the inevitable question that would come up at parties or events: "So...what are you doing now?" I couldn't really talk about *Decoded* yet, but it had been almost three years since "SWGSTBG," so I worried people would think I'd been sitting on the couch watching *Say Yes to the Dress* reruns and starting Twitter wars instead of working. The former...not true. The latter? Embarrassingly so.

Finally, we shot the first three episodes. In many ways, *Decoded* was a culmination of everything I'd been doing all along. Working at Upworthy had taught me valuable lessons about how to present serious concepts like police brutality, immigration, and racist stereotypes in ways that won't intimidate people.* And now, instead of writing in a void, I had feedback and a team. Whereas for my own YouTube videos I'd have to spend hours editing to get certain effects just right, now I could tell an editor, "Make a watermelon pop up next to my head!" and then a watermelon would pop up next to my head! I wasn't used to having someone else give me direction, but I ended up really liking that aspect, too. It was surprisingly nice to say, "Do you think this works?" and have my producer Andrew reply, "No...not at all."

The only snag was that at first I did my own makeup, and it looked absolutely terrible—my producers on *Decoded* are awesome, but I now know to never ask them if I "look all right," because "all right" is a relative term, especially when you're talking to guys who can't tell an eyeliner pencil from a stick in the ground. I acknowledged my limitations and hired Delina Medhin, a makeup artist I'd worked with on another web series, and we've been basically inseparable ever since. I was learning how to be a producer—having hard conversations about contracts,

---

* If you want to have an open conversation, start with a question. It's kind of hacky, but this way you capture people who are genuinely curious as well as people who are sure they know the answer and are mad you'd even ask. Our first episode was, "Are Fried Chicken and Watermelon Racist?"

scheduling, rates, and vision that I'd never had to have before. *Decoded* launched in June 2015, and it was a huge success—our first episode was featured on sites like the *Huffington Post* and *Adweek* with glowing reviews. The comments were so positive that I couldn't believe what was happening—it was like when you go into a café or bar and you find a door that leads to a back garden and you're like, "Wow, why is no one back here? This is great!" But I also couldn't help feeling that the positivity wouldn't last. Though this could have actually been considered my "big break," it didn't give me those delusions of grandeur I'd experienced in the past—I was too busy.

A few weeks later, Comedy Central announced that it was making a new nightly comedy show starring Larry Wilmore, the legendary producer and comedian whose résumé includes *The Fresh Prince of Bel-Air*, *The Bernie Mac Show*, *The Office*, *Black-ish*, and *Insecure*. The show would be called *The Minority Report*, and would focus on stories around race, class, and gender. I called my agent and begged him to get me an audition. I was so excited when I got word that I'd be given a shot...until I learned the audition was a character showcase, just like the *SNL* audition. And just like at the *SNL* audition, I totally bombed. Later there was a call for video submissions; I didn't get it then, either. Finally, when I had become resigned to the fact that the newly renamed *Nightly Show with Larry Wilmore* was not going to be my next big break, my MTV producer, Brendan, said he'd submitted my name as a guest for a roundtable discussion on the show, and they wanted me to come on.

It seemed too perfect. I would get to promote *Decoded* and have the chance to show Larry Wilmore and his team what they were missing without having to deal with the awkwardness of another audition. "Great," I said to Brendan. "What's the topic?"

"The Republican debate."

Oh, no, no, no. No! Although I'd been writing about social

justice for years, I'd never considered myself knowledgeable about politics. Even in those early days of the 2016 election season, being knowledgeable about politics was a full-time job. Especially Republican politics, with Ted Cruz questioning the need for Gay Pride parades and Ben Carson regularly sleepwalking through debates. I freaked out instantaneously. I cried—messy, hiccupping, embarrassing tears, the worst kind of tears to cry in front of your impressive and successful coworkers. I told Brendan there was no way I could converse halfway intelligently about Republican politics on TV. They would have to find someone else.

But Brendan wouldn't take no, no, no, no for an answer. "Listen," he said. "You have to do this." He promised to help me workshop some jokes beforehand and said he'd come to the taping. When he pointed out that Shonda Rhimes would also be a guest that night, I knew he was right: There was no way I could pass on this.

Just as I did in the days following my Anderson Cooper appearance, I started studying like a senior whose only hope of graduating on time is getting a perfect score on the Intro Stats exam. I read up on the candidates (all eight hundred of them), watched all the previous debates, and took pages and pages of notes. I picked out each candidate's most ridiculous platform and came up with ways to skewer them.

When the show finally taped, it was a *Scandal* how good I was. (Get it? Because...Shonda Rhimes was there...) During a break, I saw Larry lean over to Jordan Carlos, whom I'd done videos with before, and overheard him say, "Who is that girl?" And Jordan replied, "She's good, right?" I had to restrain myself from doing a celebratory dance in the studio.

Feeling like a grandma who's finally won the lottery after playing the same number for years, I left for a much-needed vacation with Patrick and some of our couple friends in Costa Rica. You won't believe what happened next.

The producers at Larry Wilmore contacted my agent and asked if I would come back on as a guest, so I left vacation early and hightailed it back to New York! Soon after that, they offered me a job as a writer and correspondent. I'd never worked in a writers' room before, making me the least-experienced member of the team. At my meeting with Larry, he asked me what I ultimately wanted to do with my career. I told him I wanted to sit in his chair someday. He said, "I think you could do it."

I quit my job at Upworthy and convinced my agents to work out a deal that allowed me to shoot *Decoded* on the weekends. The prospect of starting a new job in television terrified me, but the thought of giving up my web series felt inconceivable. This was also the period when my biggest diva* moment took place: Picture me sitting perfectly still in the makeup chair arguing with my producers about how *Decoded* wasn't going to suffer with my new job because "I work my ASS off!" while Delina is putting the finishing touches on my eyelashes. It's a little embarrassing to look back on it now, but it was one of the first times I had to put my foot down, which made me realize what it took to be a boss. Though this knowledge crystallized in a single moment, it was the culmination of years of mistakes, obstacles, successes, and Twitter beefs. I hadn't really had that kind of self-confidence before, and it felt good.

I'd already started to reach a wider audience with the launch of *Decoded*. Although we didn't talk about politics in the Republican/ Democrat sense, we talked about identity and how institutions

---

* In a Mariah Carey, ridiculous-but-I-earned-this way, not in a Naomi Campbell, throw-a-cell-phone way.

affect people. "Obama's presidency didn't end racism" isn't exactly a radical position, but the show where we discussed that topic in particular pissed people off nevertheless. And because people will always be nostalgic about MTV, connecting it to childhood and rebellion and edginess, fans resent any kind of change in programming like the one *Decoded* represents. It was the first time I was being introduced to an audience who were not at all on my side but instead *really* hated me—to the point that they were obsessed with trying to take me down.

I'd dealt with online harassment before (hello, chapter 2?), but this was a completely new level. Not only were viewers threatened by the concepts I was presenting, but they hated the idea that I was being paid and promoted by MTV. From outraged rhetorical questions like *Remember when MTV used to play music?* to the suggestion that I could have nothing to say about injustice because I was a woman who went to private school, married a white guy, and had a "cushy" job with a TV network, people came at me from all sides. I was censoring them (how?) and to top it all off I was rich (I wish). I was a symbol of the corrupt corporate media. People started petitions trying to get me fired—and to get me involuntarily committed to a mental institution (not kidding).

But it was all just a preview for what would happen when I started appearing on *The Nightly Show*. On top of the stress of producing and filming *Decoded*, dealing with harassment every day, and starting a new job where I was the least-experienced person on the team, I realized that my previous impulse to avoid talking about politics on television was spot on. The election was ramping up, and we'd usually devote about half of each week's episodes to politics, which increasingly meant half of each week's episodes were devoted to Trump. The amount of background information required to even have a basic discussion of the issues was overwhelming.

I'd endorsed Obama on my YouTube channel both times he

ran, but I'd never followed the elections aggressively. Now, all of a sudden I'd become a prominent voice in politics, at a time when anything you said opened you up to vicious criticism from every other position you could imagine and a few you had no idea existed. I voted for Bernie, but I didn't really endorse a candidate in the Democratic primary because I knew I would get picked apart for it, and my stance was "Whatever will keep Trump out of office is what we need to do." This seemed really reasonable to me. After Hillary got the nomination, I'd go on TV and say some version of: "Look—I know she's awkward and pandering and doesn't have the best record, and the *abuela* thing was very weird, but someone has to be president so we should vote for her anyway."

Finding your voice is one thing; using it is a whole 'nother animal. No matter what I said, viewers would become ENRAGED. I was SEXIST for suggesting that Hillary was not the heaven-sent conclusion of decades of feminist organizing and a perfect candidate for 2016! I was a COON for not condemning her husband's three-strikes crime bill and other atrocities against black people! I was RACIST for saying Donald Trump was unfit to be president—clearly I had some unfair bias against orange people! Often viewers would get mad that I hadn't mentioned such-and-such policy from 2004 when I had actually mentioned it, but it had been edited out. (Though I'd experienced the evil power of editing on *Anderson Live*, *The Nightly Show* was much more intense, because each night the editors would have to cut a twenty-minute roundtable discussion down to just four minutes, and they'd have to do it on a tight deadline.) No matter what I did, I couldn't stop the onslaught of harassment and anger that followed every single one of my appearances.

All the criticism was funneled through social media, which I was using all the time, during breaks or in the dressing room. I knew I should just ignore the trolls—you may notice that this is typical of me—but often the comments were so vicious that I felt I had to defend myself, or I at least wanted the catharsis of having fully explained my position. Though I had great relationships with everyone I worked with, I secretly cried in the bathroom pretty much every day. No one else was particularly engaged on social media, so they weren't targeted like I was. I saw it as part of my job to respond to messages that used the *Nightly Show* hashtag—sometimes someone would say, "I liked that new black girl, who is she?" and I'd reply, "Me!!!!! I'm the new black girl!!" which I was sure strengthened my brand.

When I went to the other writers for advice, they would say something like "That sucks, don't let it get to you!"—but of course I couldn't not let it get to me. Had that ever worked for me in the past? I'd always wanted to demonstrate the importance of dialogue, but I was giving way too much to "the conversation." It was like I was living in two worlds—the one where I was stressed but thriving in my new job that I'd worked so hard for, and the one where literally everyone in the world thought I was a "man-hating reverse racist Hillary Clinton shill."

One night, deep into the election, I cracked. Every time a staff member appeared on a panel or did a piece for the show, Larry would meet with us afterward to discuss our performance and where we thought we could improve. That night, I came off the taping feeling like I hadn't represented myself well—I didn't get a chance to say something, or I'd fumbled a point, or something, I don't remember. When Larry asked me how I thought I did, I started crying. "Please edit around me," I said, sniffling. "Just—can you cut me out of the panel completely?"

Naturally, Larry was pretty confused—I may have stumbled over the phrase "national security," but that's not the type of thing worth sobbing in front of your boss for. "I'm just so tired,"

I said. "Every time I go on the show, people attack me and say I'm the worst person ever and that they hate me and I'm the reason they're voting for Donald Trump." (Imagine me saying this in that crying voice you do when you're ashamed to be crying and don't want to have to stop for breath because you'll get snot everywhere if you do, so you say everything really fast.)

He said I had a voice and was on the show for a reason. I inspired people—maybe I didn't always inspire them to be nice and good, but I inspired them to say something, and that was powerful.

I knew what he was saying, but I also felt helpless—there was nothing I could do to stop it. If I got off social media, I'd be giving the trolls what they wanted—to drive me off the internet and away from my goals.

As I was sitting there looking pretty pathetic, Larry added, "Sometimes you're really clever on Twitter, but you give these people way too much attention."

If I had been embarrassed to be looking like an unhinged baby in front of my boss, the realization that he had seen me look like an unhinged baby online made it that much worse. Of course Larry followed me on Twitter. (He'd retweeted me a couple of times—NBD.) I felt stupid for not thinking of it before, but it wasn't until that moment that I became fully aware that he—and anyone else who might want to hire me—could see me going back and forth with assholes all day on social media. How many people had looked at my feed and thought, *Hmm...better not hire her—she's a loose cannon online*?

And then I thought, *Fuck—I respond to tweets at work.*

Before I took the job at *The Nightly Show*, I felt like I was destined to be the show's social justice secret weapon. It needed me. But as soon as I got into the writers' room, I couldn't shake the sense that I was in way over my head—the pace was so fast and everyone was so funny. Next to my coworkers, who had more traditional comedy backgrounds and would throw around references I couldn't place, I knew I was a risk; whenever other YouTube or internet celebrities would come on the show, if they didn't knock it out of the park, people on staff would make comments about how the internet was a cesspool of untalented wannabes.

These comments were never directed at me, and I'm sure the people making them weren't thinking about me when they made them, but it still made me feel even more like an imposter in their midst. "You do one viral video and you think you're a star" was a common annoyed refrain—uttered whenever the news was focused on the next Vine sensation—and I knew it described me perfectly. So when I realized Larry, and anyone else, could see me arguing with trolls on Twitter, I knew I must have seemed like a delusional viral star who couldn't hack it on "real TV." From a pure workplace-conduct standpoint, I also must have looked like I was wasting a lot of time. I'd grown so accustomed to multitasking that it'd become part of my process to loop through email, Facebook, Twitter, and Instagram while working, but to someone who's not active online, I knew I must have looked obsessed with social media. Sitting in Larry's office crying, I saw that I had brought this on myself.

The Nightly Show was canceled a couple of months before the election, and although I was spared the inevitable drama of covering the *Access Hollywood* tape or the resurgence of Her Emails, I got really depressed. I felt like Trump had emboldened the kind of trolls and racists who made entire careers out of harassing me (and since then, research has proven me right), and I had spent almost my entire time on the show feeding their negative energy. After the election, I had to leave social media altogether for about a month. On top of constant trolling, people would say things like "I hope you're happy—I voted for Trump and became a racist because of you." As if racism were a restaurant they'd been thinking of trying.

Both *Decoded* and *The Nightly Show* were huge steps in my career, not least because they showed me what happens when marginalized voices insist on going public. Even if you come in this package—a smiling, conventionally attractive black person who doesn't curse (at least not in her videos) or present "radical" viewpoints—you can't convince people who are committed to upholding oppression that you are anything but their worst nightmare. I will always be a radical leftist, the most racist person on TV, a poisoner of our youth, and a "black supremacist" (whatever that means). If anything, these bizarre perceptions of me are the exact reason I need to keep using my voice. These trolls aren't the people I need to reach—the people who could be influenced by that garbage are the ones I want to connect with.

When Trevor Noah interviewed Tomi Lahren, I thought he went really light on her. (Okay, I know what you're thinking: *A little hypocritical from someone who just spent several paragraphs ranting about how she can't please anyone?* But it's not like I tweeted at him and said he had betrayed all black people.) Still, when she started ranting about Black Lives Matter and Colin Kaepernick, he pulled an artfully subtle question out of his back pocket: "What is the right way to protest?"

It was perfect because she couldn't answer. You wear a T-shirt that says *BLM* and people get mad. You refuse to move your seat on the bus and people get mad. You do a sit-in and people get mad. No matter what you do, people who are dedicated to seeing marginalized people as second-class citizens will be upset when marginalized people insist that they are not second-class citizens.

While this is more than discouraging, the realization is also kind of liberating. It made me realize I should quit trying to please everyone and just say whatever the hell I want. Going public doesn't mean that the public gets to define you. Having an audience and a public platform has changed how I see the world—how could it not?—but I'm still the same person on TV as I am riding the subway, or waiting in line at the DMV, or locked out of my apartment in my bright orange muumuu—just with better makeup.

CHAPTER SIX

LESSONS FROM GOING PUBLIC, PART 2

Objects on Social Media Are Not as
Close as They Appear

There are many reasons to be jealous of Beyoncé. Her voice. Her career. The way she fills out a wide variety of leotards. But the biggest one, for me, is that there's so much we don't know about her life. And despite the illusions provided by gossip magazines and close textual analyses of her song lyrics, we'll likely never know more than the Queen wants us to.

The internet has given me a lot—I would have a completely different career without it. Posting videos on YouTube allowed me to sidestep a lot of barriers to entry in the entertainment business and get where I am today. But even though we've never met, many of my fans feel like they have a personal connection to me, and that has come with some unforeseen consequences. Don't get me wrong—I love my fans. They're great, funny, generous, smart, and engaged people. (Waves at beautiful person holding this book.) But I wish I'd known how the internet would change how we understand fame and success when I started posting videos back in 2006. I would have done some things differently. Or at least mentally prepared myself for the effects of going public.

Some of my audience has been following me since I was living with three roommates in Miami. They watched along when I moved in with Pat, when I got engaged in Paris, when I moved to New York, when I changed jobs. I used to shoot a lot of YouTube

103

videos in my bathroom, because the lighting was great, and apparently fans got attached to the floral shower curtain I had at the time. I have since moved on to a more subtle, less Target Back-to-College look, but I still occasionally get messages saying, "I miss that floral shower curtain!"

Think about your friends, family members, and coworkers. Would you recognize their shower curtains in a lineup? Would you recognize their *former* shower curtains in a lineup? I'm going to guess no. It's a little weird.

But it's also completely understandable. Social media has the opposite effect of that little warning on car side-view mirrors: Objects are not as close as they appear.

Another illustrative example: I once made a video with my flat-screen TV in the background, and trolls descended on the supposed hypocrisy of my being "rich." How dare I comment on social justice issues? How could I know what I was talking about if I had such a nice TV? What the video didn't show was that Patrick had woken up at five a.m. on Black Friday to buy that TV on deep discount, and the reason it was visible in that shot was because I had no other place to film—we were dealing with a relentless bedbug infestation at the time, and the rest of the apartment was covered in plastic.

I have to remind myself that I engineered this: I wanted people to pay attention to me! I showed everyone my shower curtain! But I didn't think about the implications of the shower curtain until strangers started emailing me about it at four a.m. Even accidentally sharing the tiniest details makes people feel like they know you—especially when "What's in my bag?" and closet tours are rites of YouTube passage.

Meanwhile, I have no idea what Beyoncé's bathroom looks like, and no matter how many people leave pleading comments on her occasional Instagram posts, I don't think she'll ever tell us. On some level, it doesn't matter. *Lemonade* would still be one of the most groundbreaking visual albums of all time if Beyoncé posted selfies at a Kylie Jenner pace. But I'm sure our perception of her as an artist and person would be totally different.

wwwww

When I used to fantasize about becoming a star, I only thought about the luxurious hotel rooms and glamorous outfits and invitations to exclusive events. Whenever I envisioned the fans, they would be adoring me, of course, but only when and how I wanted. Our interactions would always be gracious and pleasant, never uncomfortable or threatening. I imagined that if being recognized in public was ever annoying, it would be the kind of annoying where you secretly felt really smug about it.

That may be what it's like for Beyoncé, who has to incorporate privacy into her life much more intensely than I do. The reality for an "internet famous" person like me, however, is much more awkward. Since I am currently kinda-sorta famous—to some people, depending on their interests and media habits—I have a good amount of privacy, but people also think they are entitled to me in some way. I recently joined a private gym because people kept trying to take pictures with me when I was sweaty and gross; once, I was topless in the locker room (which was already a big deal for me) when I heard a tentative voice echo from the showers: "Excuse me . . . are you . . . Franchesca?"

On one hand, it's totally inappropriate to try to strike up a conversation with any naked stranger in the gym locker room. Like, don't ever do that. There is no scenario in which that is okay. But on the other hand, I knew I had made myself seem open and approachable online, so people assume I'm always open and approachable. When I shared that I'd moved into a new place, fans asked me to give an apartment tour; I had to draw a line. I wasn't going to give strangers access to my personal space this time around. (I'm not trying to get robbed, and besides, I really hate the rug Patrick picked out.)

Similarly, I recently decided to quit Snapchat because an acquaintance came up to me at an event and said, "Girl, I saw you crying on Snapchat, are you okay?" Then someone sent me a message asking, "Did you and Patrick break up? You haven't posted a picture of him in nine weeks!" I'd find myself in the middle of a dinner, enjoying a robust conversation about the top five flavors of LaCroix or savoring a plate of fried chicken and mushroom-rosemary waffles (sounds weird, but I'm team sweet-and-meat 4EVA), and suddenly I'd think, *Shit—I've got to capture this thing for the internet! Otherwise they won't know I did it!* I was so accustomed to giving so much of myself to strangers that I was starting to feel like I owed them something.

I think this is a symptom of a double standard for internet celebrities: The fans feel like they've given you your career—maybe they've been watching your videos for years—and so they expect something back. No matter that your work should be "repayment" enough—I occasionally still get emails along the lines of "I shared your video, so why won't you answer my thirty-paragraph email about how to make it as a YouTuber?"

I wish I could say I just wave all this off and move on, but I haven't been able to yet. I felt really guilty about quitting Snapchat, which is a pretty ridiculous sentence if you think about it for two seconds. I had a great connection with my audience there. But the vulnerability that made that connection so real and meaningful for me also opened me up to judgment and conspiracy theories I wasn't prepared for. Participating in social media had started to feel like I was putting myself in front of the paparazzi and telling the gossip magazines to have at it. Although I was ostensibly posting and commenting and checking my feeds on behalf of my fans, all the time I devoted there meant, paradoxically, that I had less energy for the creative projects those fans support me for. Having a huge following doesn't necessarily mean you have talent, or deserve your platform, and I let myself forget that for a little while. Maintaining a productive, rewarding relationship with fans doesn't require social media addiction—it calls for doing good work that people respond to.

~~~~~~~~

Beyond social media, my ambiguous level of fame has led to some weird encounters in person as well. Occasionally I'll be walking down the street, my headphones blasting, and notice some guy staring at me. My instinct, of course, is to put on my active bitch face (as opposed to my resting bitch face) and shoot him a *Don't even think about it* glare. Then he'll shyly approach and say, "Are you Franchesca Ramsey? I loved you on *The Nightly Show*!"

I don't want to discount all the support—both emotional and practical—my viewers give me every day. From sharing articles and research studies, to pointing out where I may have missed the mark on something, to inspiring me to cover certain topics or issues or offering words of encouragement after my teary Snapchats, I really cherish my relationship with my audience. It's symbiotic. After the video I made about my sexual assault went viral, a fan came up to me on the subway and said, "Oh my God, you're Franchesca Ramsey! I saw that video you made about when you were raped! Thank you so much for making it! You're so brave!" Though I felt uncomfortable that the entire subway car now knew I was a survivor, I was happy my story had moved her, and I got off at my stop and went on with my day. People often stop me and say, "You're like a big sister," or "I feel like you're my friend," which, since I'm an only child who used to struggle in the friend department, warms my heart.

The speaking gigs I have at schools and universities also keep me grounded. My first was at a local career day in Miami when I was twenty-five, and although I didn't have an agent or a job in the entertainment industry yet—I didn't even live in New York—it was the first time I saw that I had advice and inspiration to offer other people nevertheless. I talked about making YouTube videos as a jobby and creative work more generally, and seeing how the kids responded to my PowerPoint jokes about homework and Miley Cyrus (this was before her 420/twerking phase) made me realize my perspective was valuable even though I wasn't yet the household name I wanted to be.

Today, I regularly crisscross the country for the same kind of speaking gigs, and though I sometimes grumble about seven a.m. flights to freezing Minnesota, I think these are some of the most important parts of my work, not least because they force me to get out of the house, experience the wonder of changing out of my beloved muumuus, and talk to real humans. While people will sometimes tweet about my speeches afterward—in many ways, this feedback has inspired this book, because it's shown me what my audience cares about—live presentations are centered on interacting with the audience in real time, gaining that precious IRL experience that's absent when I get absorbed in Instagram notifications.

And thankfully, that IRL experience is almost always positive. Though I know some people have to imagine the audience in their underwear, I don't get nervous before public speaking like I do for auditions or even while making videos—when you're giving a speech, the audience wants you to succeed. (Otherwise, they have to sit through an excruciating talk.) As great as YouTube is, the engagement there is totally different, and especially so for me since my comments have been overrun by racist trolls. People who like my videos don't even want to jump in; they get harassed for weeks, and even months, if they dare utter, "Great vid!" So talking to a room of five hundred people and getting honest reactions and questions during and after, even when those comments are critical, is gratifying. There's a certain amount of generosity people have in person that disappears online, and I've learned that through experience. For example: In addition to the occasional brain fart, I've also had one real fart during a talk. I genuinely can't remember what school I was at—my brain has fuzzed the details in an effort to protect me from recurring humiliation—but one of my jokes is about how "Google is free twenty-four hours a day!" During this particular talk, I thought it would be funny to spin around in a circle for dramatic effect. While I was spinning a fart slipped out. I'm not sure if people were laughing at the spin, the fart, or both, but I swear it felt like my ass had been handed a megaphone; it was not one of those dainty accidental squeaks. It was toward the end of my speech, so I didn't acknowledge it and neither did anyone else, for which I'm very grateful.

So like I said, this kind of thing keeps me grounded. For every diva moment, or time I'm recognized on the street, there's some other time I fall flat on my face, exposing myself to be a victim of the same celebrity culture that means I have to pay a hundred dollars more per month to go to the gym. (Yes—New York is expensive.) The best example of this was when I met up with Tracee Ellis Ross—okay, I'm name-dropping, but I promise there's a point!—in LA to shoot a video for my channel with her. We were filming at a hotel, and when we wrapped up we went out for lunch. As we were leaving the restaurant, a handsome black guy with locs came up to us and gushed, "I just wanna tell you: I'm such a fan."

Maybe it was his locs, or maybe you can chalk up my smugness to being in LA and hanging with one of my favorite actresses, but instantly my face lit up. "Oh, thank you so much!" I said, going into my Gracious Celebrity mode. I may have flipped my hair over my shoulder. "What's your name?"

He stared at me for a second before angling his body away from the embarrassing moment I'd just created. "Thanks so much," Tracee said. "It was great to meet you!" he said, and quickly walked off. He was—obviously—talking to the network television star standing next to me.

CHAPTER SEVEN
GUESS WHO'S COMING TO DINNER? (IT'S LENA DUNHAM.)

Like many viewers, when HBO's series *Girls* debuted, I quickly began to treat Hannah Horvath and Lena Dunham, the actress who played her, as well as the show's creator, as one and the same. From her tone-deaf blunders to the way she was constantly disrobing onscreen, Hannah was ignorant, narcissistic, and just plain obnoxious, and she infuriated me. I responded by trashing the show in a series of TV recaps I made for YouTube with my best friend, De'Lon. *Does the world need yet another show about rich white girls in New York who don't take the subway, live in giant apartments, and have lots of sex? The answer is no. We already had* Sex and the City, *which was infinitely better in terms of both writing and outfits.*

Because Lena Dunham was the showrunner, creator, and star of *Girls*—and because she seemed unable to resist making dumb comments in interviews and all over social media—a lot of my criticism focused on her. While many people were vocally annoyed by Dunham and her work on *Girls*, I was *really* annoyed. Of course, I could have spent the time and energy I wasted hate-watching and then panning this show doing productive or valuable things, but instead I tuned in every week so that I could make myself feel better about having a less successful acting career than Lena. Some people do really in-depth, nuanced TV recaps; this was not what De'Lon and I were making. Sure, we discussed the lack of diversity on the show, and dissected Lena's repeated missteps when it came to race beyond the series. But overall, our criticisms were snarky and mean. Although we never called Lena fat outright, we would happily skirt the line and say shaming things like, "Why can't she keep her clothes on?" and "Girl, that dress does not fit, and you look like a mess."

I didn't think about it at the time, but the old maxim about how there's no such thing as bad press really applies here: We were basically promoting the show. People would comment that they'd never heard of *Girls* before they saw my videos, but our reviews were so hilarious and biting that their interests were piqued. Could the show really be as bad as we claimed? We assured them it was, but my subscribers set their DVRs to find out for themselves anyway. Still, we soldiered on, as if roasting a person that everyone else was already roasting were our civic duty.

The beginning of the second season of *Girls* was when we really hit our stride, thanks to a little help from Lena's terrible PR responses. After a totally white season one, Lena and her co-showrunner, Jenni Konner, had responded to extensive criticism of the show's lack of diversity by plopping Donald Glover in as a walk-on love interest at the start of season two. Unfortunately, his character was a Republican who didn't think Hannah's writing was good, so she dumped him, meaning we saw him in all his shirtless handsome glory for only two measly episodes. I'll admit, I was jealous of those sex scenes, which resulted in me taking subtle digs at Lena with comments like, "In what world would Donald Glover ever sleep with Lena Dunham?" As if he would ever slide into *my* DMs.

Lena's track record on discussing race wasn't stellar pre-*Girls*. She'd gotten flack for saying she had "yellowish fever," along with making a number of infantilizing comments about Asian women, in a travel essay about Japan. She'd donned a fake burka on her Instagram and bragged about being considered "thin in Detroit." (After we stopped doing recaps, she endured other controversies related to her book that I won't get into.) Suffice to say she was "embattled" in the media, which I thought gave me a free pass to say whatever I wanted about her. And while I didn't mince words, my rationale was "The truth hurts, and it's funny as hell," so I failed to see a problem.

Around this time, an internet friend I'd become close with told me she was coming to New York and invited me to a dinner she was having. We'd never met in person, so I excitedly agreed. There would be a group of people at the dinner, which meant it would probably be one of those ambiguous work/friends things where you get to network without feeling (too) sleazy.

Until the day approached, I didn't think too much about it. But then, a few hours before we were supposed to meet, I got a text from my friend explaining that the restaurant was cash only—and she added that it was "Lena's favorite place." Her comment was so casual that I didn't want to out myself as clueless by asking, "Lena who?" Instead, I did some internet sleuthing (combing through Twitter mentions and tagged Instagram photos) and deduced she must have meant Lena Dunham. Which meant that Lena Dunham would be in attendance that evening. *Shit.*

I started to panic. Would my friend have told her who would be at the dinner in advance? Would Lena look me up? And if she did, was she the kind of person who would Google "Franchesca Ramsey + Lena Dunham" just to see if anything came back? I tried to tell myself that I was overstating my importance to Lena Dunham and that there was no way she would come into this dinner looking for a fight. *She's, like, an actual famous person*, I reasoned. *She doesn't have time to Google random plebes she's having dinner with. Does she???*

At the restaurant, the scene was much more intimate than I expected—not a huge group dinner like your most popular friend's birthday. We were all sitting in a booth. Naturally, because that's how the universe works, I ended up sitting next to Lena.

I felt mortified, but she didn't seem to notice—she didn't know who I was. She was so nice, encouraging, and curious; nothing about her was "catty," or disengaged, or straight-up mean. She asked me what I did, and we got to talking about the internet. I had been dealing with a lot of harassment on social media at the time, and we bonded over how awful people can be—you know, classic girl talk. She showed me her Twitter mentions, which were a whole 'nother level, like nothing I'd ever seen or experienced. A constant stream of "I wish you'd get raped" and "I wish someone would murder you"—and she hadn't even said or done anything that day! Though there was some genuine, well-meaning critique mixed in, it was pretty much drowned out by the awful name-calling. Sometimes in the exact same tweet.

I remembered vividly how I felt after my *Anderson Live* appearance, when hordes of strangers descended on all my public accounts to attack me from every side. My stomach sank. If she had as good a time as I did, she would probably go home and look me up, and she would think I was a two-faced jerk. I couldn't leave without coming clean. "Listen," I said, "can I be totally honest with you?" I took a deep breath. "I've never been a fan of yours."

This is not usually the kind of thing you hear from someone you just met—or, really, from anyone—so I imagine she was a little confused, though maybe she gets it all the time. I went on. "I mean, I've been pretty vocal about not liking you. But you seem cool, and I don't feel good about some of the things I've said, so I feel like I need to be honest with you. If you go online and look me up, you'll probably find me talking about how much *Girls* sucks."

She was gracious—I mean, as much as you could be in that situation. She thanked me for telling her and said she understood the criticisms, that she was really trying to expand her worldview and understand her privilege. We exchanged numbers and left on a good note.

Then, later that night, she texted me something along the lines of "Wow. So...you really hate me! You hate me a lot!"

I felt so bad. I explained that I didn't hate her, but I never thought I'd meet her, and when you don't have to think about the real human behind the celebrity gossip, it's easy to get caught up in the drama. Then, because I felt like I'd learned an important lesson that night, I asked Lena if she would be okay with me writing about the experience for my Tumblr, and she agreed.

Writing about it forced me to ask myself why I had such deep problems with this woman. Though some of my issues with her work were valid, I had to admit that many of my critiques were rooted in my own insecurities about my career—if I were being honest. I'd spent most of 2012 developing a pitch for HBO that was ultimately rejected as "too network." I'd wondered if that meant "not enough boobs." Personally, I had always been self-conscious about my body—I no doubt would've sobbed my way through an on-screen second base, much less the scene where Adam pees on Hannah in the shower. (Ew.) It was easier to dismiss her work—which has had positive effects, like hugely advancing the body-positivity movement and awareness of reproductive rights—than to say I was intimidated and a little jealous.

The thesis of my Tumblr post boiled down to: If you participate in the shit-slinging contest, competing to come up with the most creative insult, you end up covered in shit. I didn't want to excuse the real problems Lena had, but I'd let bigotry get in the way of my criticisms, and it wasn't something I felt good about. I topped off my post with a photo of me and Lena at the restaurant and waited for everyone to appreciate how wise and mature I was being. Once again, I was wrong. "This sounds like extreme white apologism and it kinda makes my stomach turn crazy," one Tumblr user responded. "You're in with whites and now have some social capital and you're telling us how to approach it? I'm sorry this whole writing just made you look like a complete coward."

"Racist white person knows you don't like her so to seem less racist, she acts a little less pretentious because she knows you're going to blog about her. And we're supposed to give her and other racist celebrities the benefit of the doubt and speak nicely because .??" wrote another.

"Chescaleigh, girl... Like I know we all gotta play the game sometimes to get what we want but us regular Blacks don't have time or energy to speak or play nice."

I had told an award-winning actress, to her face, that I didn't like her, which I'm pretty sure is the exact opposite of cowardice. Not to mention I'd ordered the most inexpensive item on the menu at dinner at a fairly fancy restaurant, which felt very "regular" to me. Whatever that meant. It's not like I had written, "Anyone who calls out Lena Dunham for anything is a despicable human who should feel ashamed. #TeamLena!"

Yet I was accused of sucking up to her so I would get a part on *Girls*, while other critics went more the "Speak for yourself, I was *never* jealous of Lena" route. Never mind that I *was* speaking for myself—I thought the frequent use of the word "I" would signify that. Still others thought I had "betrayed" them—but could they really be surprised, given that I went to Catholic school, had a white husband, and screwed up my appearance on *Anderson Live*? I was, in their eyes, "canceled," never to be taken seriously again.

I'll stand by it: I don't think I did anything wrong with my post. I absolutely think Lena—like anyone else—should continue to be called out for the ignorant things she says and does. (Remember when she put all kinds of sexist words in Odell Beckham Jr.'s mouth because he didn't hit on her at the Met Gala? Come on!) I get why people dislike Lena Dunham; her daily mantra should be, "Did anyone ask for your opinion?" She desperately needs a private journal. I even had some anxiety about telling this story because I don't want it to seem like I'm defending her. But her textbook white feminism doesn't mean I should sacrifice my morals to criticize her. There's no value in peppering critique with stigmatizing personal attacks. When you add, "P.S. You're fat," to a criticism about the way a person has handled—or ignored—race on her television show, for example, you negate the power of the original idea. It's like adding vinegar to a perfectly good birthday cake. (Let's ignore for a minute that there's nothing wrong with being fat, because we all know the pain that postscript is meant to inflict.) The person on the receiving end will only hear the personal attack, and will probably write off the legitimate criticism as part of a cruel attempt to insult and humiliate. On top of that, anyone else in the world who may identify with the personal attack is going to feel bad.

Ultimately, this story isn't about Lena Dunham. It's about holding yourself to a high standard no matter how terrible the person you're calling out may be. I'm not saying that everyone deserves the benefit of the doubt—not at all. Nor do I think callouts should revolve around the feelings of the person on the other end. But being held accountable for how your words or actions were intentionally or unintentionally oppressive is uncomfortable enough without devolving into a cheap Fashion Police aftershow. Bigotry has no place in our callouts, but we see it show up all the time. When someone makes a homophobic comment, some argue, "I'm sure he's overcompensating because he's gay." When a woman has really bad politics, people will say, "She looks like a man in a skirt." I'd rather focus my energy highlighting what someone said or what they did—remembering, all the while, that there are consequences when your criticisms of horrible actions are draped in the bigotry you're trying to speak out against. (And I know all too well how it feels to discover an entire thread on a forum dedicated to debating whether or not you have an ass. I do squats!)

It's really hard to take the high road when you're calling out someone who's truly awful. A good example of this is Donald Trump's allegedly small penis, which many people liked to mock in the months leading up to the election, before he had the nuclear codes. Let me put it plainly: Fuck Donald Trump and his rampant racism, sexism, xenophobia, Nazi apologism, climate-change denial, and unending desire to send our country and the entire world straight to hell in a handbasket decorated with a Confederate-flag pattern. Seriously. But the possibility of him having a tiny penis has nothing to do with his bigotry. We already live in a world that constantly links penis size to wealth, success, and sexual prowess when none of those things are related.

I once read an article that made the point that when you call out a racist family member over Thanksgiving dinner, your words aren't aimed solely at that family member. They're aimed at everyone else at the table, who may benefit from hearing what you have to say, as well. I'd say the same goes for all of us when we call someone out online. Who's at the table? Maybe someone who's struggling to accept the body they were given will stumble on your insensitive joke and miss the bigger message. And you never know who might be invited to dinner next.

CHAPTER EIGHT

STOP HATING AND START STUDYING

I'm extremely flattered/slightly embarrassed when people describe me as a "super-woke black feminist queen."*†‡§ But as often as I'm praised for the conversations my content has sparked online, I'm far from everyone's cup of tea. A quick Google search of my name will bring up my YouTube channel, episodes of *Decoded*, and clips from *The Nightly Show*, but as you scroll farther and farther, the results get weirder and weirder. Petitions to get me fired or involuntarily committed. Supercuts of weird faces I've made in videos, video game walk-throughs in which players attempt to kill characters they think look like me, and shitty memes calling me some variation of a "racist cunt." There are videos in which men—it's usually men—rant for nearly an hour about how I don't understand what "political correctness" means. Some of these videos have hundreds of thousands or even millions of views; since I've gone viral myself, I know that equals a nice paycheck. People have made entire careers out of hating me.

When friends or colleagues stumble onto this treasure trove of hateful content, the first thing they ask is how I handle it. I don't tell them how often I cry to my husband or how I set up filters for

---

*   Yes, they do.
†   I'm serious, they do.
‡   They do!
§   Okay…maybe the "queen" part is optional.

racial slurs across my email and social media. Instead I give them the short answer: I remind myself that the types of people who invest time in hating me are largely fueled by racism and sexism, with a heaping dose of jealousy.

The racism and sexism are pretty obvious with the folks throwing "black supremacist cunt" around. But how am I so sure jealousy is to blame for the rest? Well, I used to be a hater myself. [*Cue dramatic organ music.*]

Now, before you go chucking this book out a window, feeling a deep sense of betrayal and disappointment: Please don't litter, and please allow me to explain.

Long before I moved to New York, I followed a Manhattan socialite and new-media personality whose career I not-so-secretly envied and whose personal life I found not-so-secretly fascinating. Let's call her Stephanie. Stephanie had rich parents, a cushy job at a gossip magazine, a marginally successful pop culture web series, a pilot in development, and a couples' blog with her boyfriend that was a total disaster. She went out a lot and wrote an advice column in which she'd tell people things like "If you want to save money, stop going to the Hamptons!" She inspired in me a precise combination of aspiration and disgust, and I was nothing short of obsessed with her. While some people flock to trashy reality shows for their judgmental voyeuristic kicks, I was refreshing Tumblr during work hours, wondering what Stephanie was up to.

When I first discovered Stephanie, I was living in Miami, working as a graphic designer and only dabbling in the entertainment industry through my YouTube videos and cringeworthy stand-up sets—let's just say my closer was a JonBenét Ramsey joke…and it brought the house down every time. I had a lot of time to follow this woman's life. On her Tumblr, she'd amassed a moderate following, as well as an active commenting community filled with fans, spectators, and haters. I drifted among all three camps, but I skewed toward the hater category. I imagined she'd had everything handed to her, and it really irritated me. Why couldn't someone hand everything to me?

After a few months of enduring the public's vicious analysis of her posts, Stephanie closed her comments section. This act of self-preservation galvanized us lovers/haters to take our fixation to the next level. She had decided to prevent us from interacting with her directly... but that kind of felt like she had given us permission to go off into the wild frontier and drag her in ways we might have been hesitant about if we knew she was going to see it. We all packed up and started a new site dedicated to gossiping and theorizing about whatever Stephanie posted. Although I'd been living with my serious boyfriend for years, we affectionately called ourselves "pathetic virgins"—because only lonely ladies who've never gotten laid would spend so much time gossiping about a complete stranger online. Look at us being all self-deprecating and totally not weird! Cool, huh?

In an effort to set ourselves apart from Stephanie's "comment section dictatorship," we decided nothing in the way of snark was off-limits on our site. The only rule was "Don't poke the beast," which meant that we agreed not to contact Stephanie or taunt her into reading our posts. (But it was totally acceptable to call her a beast. Sheesh.) The site was supposed to be our space—and while no one held back with the insults, we agreed that flinging them directly at Stephanie was a line that shouldn't be crossed. It was entertaining at first, like we were a panel of judges on a reality TV show, and even though I never said anything quite as awful as some of the other members, I enjoyed watching it all unfold. It felt righteous and cathartic to shit-talk this rich media darling while I was struggling to get a job and pay rent.

If this sounds "so high school," that's because high school is where you learn this kind of behavior. Around ninth grade, right when I started feeling insecure about my body and lack of popularity, I discovered I was funny, and I started using my humor as a shield. I was particularly self-conscious about my lopsided boobs (which I now know are totally normal), so I attempted to conceal them by wearing a thick orange foam bra insert. I stressed about it constantly. I assumed everyone could see the orange cutlet, and I would bolt indoors at the slightest sign of rain for fear that my foam boob would take on water like the *Titanic* and reveal my secret. Cracking jokes at the expense of others became an easy way to gain friends and divert attention away from myself and my own insecurities. I remember once helping spread a rumor that a girl in my class had an extra toe, which resulted in an endless stream of bad foot puns and jokes about a supposed "sixth sense." I went on the attack instead of showing compassion for a classmate who may or may not have had an extra digit; I distracted from my own body-image issues by starting rumors about someone else's. Although I had never met Stephanie and she had never done anything to me, I was responding to her in a similar way: I was insecure about my career, so I took it out on someone whose career reminded me of all the ways I wasn't succeeding. You could say I was using my powers for evil.

We spent so much time on the pathetic virgins forum that we soon began to discuss topics beyond Stephanie's awful New Year's Eve party outfit and whether her parents were still paying her rent. We had conversations about books, music, food, life. Soon our group started to feel like a dinner party filled with old friends. I had finally moved to New York, and while I was struggling to meet people and figure out how to pursue my dreams in real life, it felt good to have a place to vent and crack jokes among like-minded strangers.

During one particularly depressing stretch, I found the nerve to share with the group that I was going through an especially hard time and struggling. I'd talked to my boyfriend and best friend about it at the time, but I didn't feel like I was getting the support I needed. (Then again, I didn't really know what I needed.) When I posted about my feelings on the site, members leaped into action, sharing their stories and offering encouragement. One woman messaged me privately and when we met up for coffee she didn't even blink when I cried on her shoulder. I even picked up freelance graphic design work from a few members after complaining about my degree collecting dust while I folded clothes at Anthropologie.

So it wasn't all bad. But mostly it was. It felt good to be part of a "club"—I imagine a lot of online trolls feel this way, too—so I excused any particularly egregious, offensive comments (about how Stephanie was fat or "looked like a man") in exchange for my membership. I tried to focus on the few and far-between positives. When the site moderators announced they would host a meetup in New York, I decided to go.

Making the leap from online to offline friendship is always risky, but with a few positive pathetic virgin encounters under my belt, I thought, *What's the worst that could happen?* I made the hour-long trek from Queens to a dive bar in Brooklyn and discovered I'd joined a *Mean Girls*–style clique. If you've ever made a friend online, you understand the intensity of that kind of friendship—it's no less "real" than a friendship with someone you met at school or work. I assumed that my fellow PVs would be less snarky in real life and more like the kinds of people I'd want to hang with on the regular.

But the whole thing felt blatantly uncool. I had assumed Stephanie would be the unspoken elephant/beast in the room. We'd act as if we'd known each other for ages in between knowing winks and inside jokes. Instead, they wouldn't stop talking about Stephanie. Things got even stranger when one of the moderators—let's call her xXJosieCatXx—latched on to me as if we'd been friends forever. This wouldn't have been so strange—we'd spent years palling around online together—if JosieCat hadn't been so nasty to me in the months and years we'd spent on the site. When one of the other PVs discovered my YouTube channel, JosieCat had called me out as being "just jealous" of Stephanie. Which I was, but so was everyone else—that was why we'd established an entire website to make fun of her? Naturally, I was a little nervous to meet JosieCat face-to-face, but instead of delivering cutting insults, she wouldn't stop fawning all over me. She paraded me around the bar, asking people if they'd met me or watched my hilllaaaaarious videos.

Though now I'm more familiar with the ways people's personalities shift when they close their laptops and get out into the real world, it felt completely bizarre, and embarrassing at the time. It suddenly became very clear how much time I'd wasted with these people. Instead of working on videos, or taking an acting class, or doing literally anything valuable, I'd spent a significant portion of my life for the past two years coming up with mean conspiracy theories about a D-list New York media celebrity who was off partying and booking gigs while I made jokes about becoming an old spinster with no one to cuddle but her cats. And I really don't like cats.

I wish I could say that this period of my life gave me the good sense to go easy on the haterade. But although it gave me perspective on how people who are unhappy offline can project their negative feelings onto someone else, I'm sorry to say it took another slap in the face to make me go cold turkey.

After "SWGSTBG," I used some of the money I earned to go to a fancy tech conference. I'd never been to anything like it before, and I was excited to meet many of my internet friends (and, okay, I was also excited to show off in the wake of my viral hit). While there, I met a really successful YouTuber whom I'd taken to casually trashing in my group texts between internet friends. I'd never really "gotten" her success—I didn't think she was particularly funny or charismatic. I couldn't understand why she had all these fans and opportunities and I didn't. In other words, I was jealous.

One night, when we ended up at the same party, I was shocked when she introduced herself and said she was a fan of my work. She was so gracious, charming, and generous that my envy melted away. Eventually the conversation turned to dealing with anxiety, and I stood there puzzled by the thought that someone who appeared so happy and successful could possibly struggle with panic attacks and self-doubt, just like I did. I somehow got up the nerve to share that my anxiety was particularly bad before auditions; I'd find any excuse to put off learning my lines, and too many times I'd email my agent with some excuse about why I couldn't make the audition. I would also get really nervous about having to make videos regularly, which meant I would get into my own head and put things off till the last minute. Procrastination had become my coping mechanism. That way when I bombed the audition, or the video wasn't as good as it could have been, I had an excuse: I hadn't had enough time to try my best. So the failure wasn't my fault.

She told me something that has changed the way I think to this day: Look at your work as a contract you have with yourself. Getting auditions is work. Posting videos is work. Even if you don't book the gig or go viral, you've still met the conditions of your contract. As with any job, you don't just sit around achieving all day—you have to put in hours. Until that point, whenever I saw someone doing something I wanted to do, I'd devote many of those hours to negative energy. I would try to convince myself that these strangers weren't worthy of the things I wanted instead of being honest with myself about how they got there.

Even spoiled Stephanie had to put in some amount of work. Even if you have all the connections in the world, you still have to show up and do the work. More often than not, I couldn't even manage to show up.

In that moment, I realized I'd been going about my career all wrong. Instead of hating, I should've been studying.

Now we're at the part of the chapter where I say the internet has made all this stuff worse. The internet has made all this stuff worse! Jealousy is human nature, and although every industry is built on competition, entertainment and media are particularly cutthroat. There's always been this idea that there are only so many fans to go around, only so many slots for people to fit into. The internet has only heightened this problem: From the perspective of a creator, social media allows us to present ourselves as much more successful and interesting than we really are. The illusion of our interesting success begets more fans, which then creates the illusion that we are *even more* interesting and successful. From the perspective of a wannabe creator, social media is a great way to take the focus off what you need to work on and instead funnel all your energy into the pointless project of hating.

After realizing my life as a hater was turning me into a resentful jerk, I decided to stop hating and start studying—and I don't just mean studying my enemies' Instagram accounts, though I still go down the "Tagged Photo" rabbit hole occasionally. I started paying closer attention to the YouTubers, actors, and creators whom I envied/admired, watching what they were doing, and what I wasn't. They took improv classes. They worked out. So I upped the gym time—which had the bonus of helping with my anxiety—got new head shots, took a hosting class, and stopped going out as much. Every day, I asked myself: How do I get the things in my career that I want but don't have? What do I do to get them?

But channeling the green-eyed monster into productivity is especially difficult when there are temptations every time you open your computer. There's that saying "If you have haters, then you're doing something right," but I disagree—at this point, if you have haters you're doing anything. I have a feeling that the caveman who discovered fire had a few cave folks rolling their eyes while happily huddled by the blaze. You can get a job—any job—and the sassiest member of your extended family will comment on your celebratory Facebook post with "Uh-huh, I see you, you think you're hot stuff with your li'l job now." Point is, having haters doesn't mean you're "winning." It doesn't mean you're doing something inherently abhorrent, either. It just means that you shouldn't put too much stock in them. I know that's easier said than done. (Hello! I've literally written a book about it.) With all the ways for people to invade your life via inbox, petty jealousies and snarky comments can feel really personal. But there are always going to be people who don't like you, and you can't be friends with everyone. Whatever you do, someone, somewhere, is going to disapprove.

While I truly believe a little saltiness is natural (and at times amusing), it's what we do with that flavorful seasoning that matters. Setting aside the case of contact that the internet allows, hating in itself is pretty harmless. Waste of time? Sure. Pathetic? Guilty. But in most cases (as it was in those heady days before the advent of Twitter mentions), the "hatee" isn't directly affected, because they have no idea their haters even exist. Once, I was riding home from church with my grandmother (who is hands down the most hilariously shady woman I know) when Vanessa Williams's "Save the Best for Last" came on the radio. Right as

I was getting ready to belt, "Sometimes the snow comes down in June," my grandmother growled, "And sometimes you should stick to acting." Sick burn, Grandma, but damn—she's no Whitney or Mariah, but I always thought Vanessa's voice was cute! Plus, she had some hits! Anyway, while I sat there dumbfounded, guess what Vanessa Williams did? Went about her business, losing not a single night of sleep over my grandma's shade.

These days, however, it's not enough for some people to deride your achievements and make fun of your questionable singing abilities from afar. No, now many haters will take it to the next level, because just as the internet allows you to present your life exactly how you want it to look, it also gives you easy, direct access to the people you're hating on—from Anne Hathaway (what did she ever do?) to those twelve-year-old girls on *Dance Moms*. As my profile rises, the kind of negative attention I attract makes me realize what I could have become if I'd let my hatred get out of hand: a troll.

The natural extension of the hater, the troll is not satisfied with merely disliking you—they want to keep you from doing anything but listening to their complaints. They want to distract you, suck up your time and energy, and then, having sapped you of your creative forces, drag you down to their lair, where they will make you watch *The Big Bang Theory* until you start making jokes about how it's kinda fucked up that women won't sleep with nice guys. When you get a new car, trolls don't just say, "Well, well, well—Franchesca must think she's something with her new little car"—they email you and say, "Hey bitch, your car is trash, and I know where you parked it."

The moment when I realized that the YouTuber I frequently shit-talked was just a normal person who worked very hard was a turning point, steering me away from the path that leads under the bridge, so to speak. Thinking about how lucky I was to have met her in person showed me how to deal with my jealousy in a constructive way, by channeling that energy into the things I wanted to improve about my career. I wish the same were true of my trolls, especially the men—there's something about a black woman being successful and happy that infuriates white men in particular. They have all this privilege, but they still feel sad or lonely or frustrated or whatever—so how dare *I* not feel sad or lonely or frustrated?

If these guys invested half the time they spend trying to ruin my life and put it into their own careers, they might feel better. Why not take those twenty different vivid metaphors for how much they hate me and turn them into a novel? The detective work they expend looking up the contact information for my agent, my manager, the schools I'm speaking at, and my boss at MTV so they can tell them to fire me could be translated into a really promising career in PR. Signing my podcast-contact email up for porn newsletters and weird coupons for hemorrhoid cream are examples of creativity—the kind of creativity they might put toward creating a writing sample for any number of late-night television shows or network comedies instead of wasting their lives responding to YouTube comments in a blind rage.

Unfortunately, the trolls are too short-sighted, or too bitter, to channel their negative energy into something positive, so they let it seep out into the world instead.

The most impressive/horrifying are the guys who make videos about me. It's not enough for them to just post a rant about how much they hate me—they have to make a fifty-minute video about how much they hate me, email it to me, and ask me to watch it. For those who have never made forays into the YouTube world, a fifty-minute video takes a lot of time to make—these aren't just webcam rants filmed in front of a white wall. They're often fully produced videos, with costumes and skits and graphics and multiple actors. I'll admit I've not only watched some of these horrid videos, but even found myself thinking, *That animation is actually not too bad?*

One guy in particular has made a number of videos about me. That number being around forty, including a musical. He's mocked my stances on topics that range from political correctness to voting rights and made crude jokes about my husband. His videos attempt to take down a wide variety of what he calls "social justice warriors," but he seems to have a particular fascination with me. Usually his comments are stupid; sometimes they're scary. Every time he posts something about me, I get a barrage of hate from copycat fans who send me vile messages so they can screenshot them and impress all the other trolls.

So last year, naturally, I decided that I would meet him.

If you're familiar with the writer Lindy West's work, you may recognize this impulse from her *This American Life* episode "If You Don't Have Anything Nice to Say, SAY IT IN ALL CAPS." I was listening to it while grocery shopping and burst into tears in the cereal aisle—I hadn't realized how much my trolls were getting to me, and her experience really resonated. In the piece, Lindy describes a particularly cruel troll who created a fake Twitter account impersonating her dead father. Ignoring the online-woman's maxim to "never feed the trolls," she wrote an article for *Jezebel* explaining why the abuse hurt. Then the troll did the unthinkable: He emailed her to confess all the ways he'd trolled her, and he apologized. "I don't know why or even when I started trolling you," he wrote. "I think my anger towards you stems from your happiness with your own being. It offended me because it served to highlight my unhappiness with my own self." About a year later, hoping to learn more about the motivations of trolls, she reached out asking if he'd have a conversation with her for the radio show.

The results were illuminating, humanizing, and frankly incredible, and I wanted to replicate them with my own dedicated trolls—at least those who never bothered to conceal their identities, making it easy for me to contact one of them. I knew we would both be at VidCon, the annual online video conference held in Southern California, that year, and after exchanging a few tweets, we agreed to sit down together.

Patrick begged me not to do it, and in hindsight I should have listened to him. But in my heart, I wanted to believe that people aren't just all good or all bad. Because I'd spent years as a hater myself, I was willing to believe my troll was more than the nasty stuff he posted online. I knew he had a girlfriend, parents, and people in his life who think he's great. Maybe they think the troll-y YouTube videos don't represent who he is. Maybe they don't even watch them!

I should have remembered that you can't reason with people whose whole purpose is to get your attention and distract you. When your adversary is someone who has serious issues to work through, it doesn't matter how smart your comeback is or how sympathetic and honest you are—you just can't win.

The experience of meeting this troll at VidCon was not unlike what happened when I met JosieCat, the salty moderator from the pathetic virgin forum: Instead of looking me up and down like he was Meryl Streep in *The Devil Wears Prada*, or asking me if I called my husband a racist in bed, or dumping a bucket of pig's blood on my head as I crossed the threshold, this guy basically groveled. He said he was so sorry for all the abuse he'd given me, that he respected me, and that he hoped we could move on from our differences and be friends. He also confessed a bunch of personal stuff that he used to explain where his anger came from.

I was really taken aback. All I wanted to say was that he had misconstrued my work and put a bunch of words in my mouth, and to show him that I'm a real person and that his actions have consequences. I mentioned that whenever he made videos it would set off a ripple effect with his fans, who would attempt to contact me with even more aggressive messages than what this guy's video contained, and that it really upset me. I made it clear that I wasn't trying to be his therapist, or his friend, and that I appreciated his apology but really just wanted the harassment to stop.

We left on decent terms, and I thought it was possible things would get better. But of course the guy made a video about how we'd met and worked out all our problems and were now on our way to being closer than Snoop Dogg and Martha Stewart. I should have known he'd do this; hating me was part of his career, and he couldn't resist the opportunity to cook this grade-A beef.

I sort of understood his desire to say we'd become the best of friends, and I didn't really want to start another confrontation by shutting it down; plus, it made him look good, or at least like his behavior wasn't irredeemable. And it wasn't so different from the cinematic resolution to our entirely one-sided feud that I'd envisioned, though in my version I was more like a benevolent queen lording my power over him before saying it was behind us—as long as he never trolled again.

But something about his suggestion that we were equals who had put our differences aside got to me. This guy made forty videos about how I'm the scum of the earth, and I'm supposed to forgive him because he said he was sorry? I'm supposed to consider him my friend? I would have a hard time forgiving my own mother if she did that to me. His new video made me realize he hadn't earned the benefit of the doubt.

Fuming, I went on *Last Name Basis*, the podcast I host with Pat, and talked shit. I didn't name the troll, or say anything specific about our meeting, but I did say some nasty stuff that I'm not proud of, calling anti-feminists ugly and trotting out harmful stereotypes by saying that the guy and his fans probably needed to get laid. I don't know why I assumed he didn't listen to my podcast, but of course he did, and sure enough, another video appeared, about how "Racist Franny" was a duplicitous snake in the grass who had betrayed a man who thought they were friends. He then hosted a two-hour live stream dedicated to listening and reacting to the twelve-minute segment of my podcast and encouraging his fans to pile on with him. His fans used the incident to make him out to be a victim, and now we're back where we started. (His followers were sending me snake emojis long before Taylor Swift decided to embrace that as her brand.) Or actually even further behind where we started, because now he and his fans believe I attacked them.

So, to recap, here are all the mistakes I made in this situation: First, I tried to meet a troll and reason with him. Second, I thought some sense of closure would come out of this meeting based on one extraordinary news story that bore some similarities to my troll situation but actually, in retrospect, not very many. (My troll never reached out to me to apologize—I reached out to him.) Third, I got mad about the guy's reaction to the meeting we shouldn't have had and "fed the troll" by ranting about it on my podcast. Fourth, I broke my own rule about criticism, venturing into bigotry rather than attacking what he'd said and done. I pushed myself to let go of the situation when I wasn't ready, and I made the whole thing worse.

Whether you're the hater or the hated, the troll or the trolled, we could all be smarter about how we respond to natural feelings of jealousy and how they spill out on the internet. I sometimes wonder how much farther along in my career I'd be if I hadn't dedicated so much time and energy to these people. The loudest voices are distracting, but they're not necessarily the majority, and giving so much to them was doing my actual fans a disservice. (This is also why I've pulled back from social media lately: Not only has it made a huge difference for my productivity—obviously—but it's also allowed me to reframe my goals and priorities.)

When you see someone doing something you wish you could do, or achieving success you wish you could achieve, don't sit around making memes about how your dog could paint better than this girl—get your ass in the studio. (Hopefully one without internet access.) And when your work starts selling for hundreds of dollars, and then thousands of dollars, and someone starts making videos of his dog stepping in paint, walking on a canvas, and saying, "Look—my dog made a better painting than Kim Jenkins," just ignore it. His landlord is going to have a field day over the blue paw prints in the carpet.

HATERS VERSUS TROLLS: A GUIDE

There's a big difference between being a hater like sweet, young Franchesca and a full-blown Breitbart employee. Hating is not productive, but it's mostly harmless, especially if you're focused on a celebrity. They don't have time for you. Trolling helped elect Donald Trump, and contributes to thousands of women and marginalized people feeling unsafe every day. Now that you've learned all about what not to do when you encounter a hater or troll, I've made a handy chart to help you spot them.

HATERS vs TROLLS

	HATERS	TROLLS
MODE of ATTACK	Gossip, subtweets	Articles, videos, @-replies, emails, emails to people close to you—basically anything they can get their hands on
GOAL	Catharsis	Attention
CELEBRITY MASCOT	Taylor Swift	Donald Trump
FAVORITE "CELEBRITIES"	*Real Housewives of [Insert Location Here]*, the Kardashians, *Love & Hip Hop [Insert Location Here]*	Alex Jones of Infowars, Tomi Lahren, self-described "anti-Social Justice Warriors"
FAVORITE MEDIA SCANDAL	Kylie Jenner's pregnancy	GamerGate
FAVORITE BEVERAGE	Tea	Bitters

CHAPTER NINE

ACTIVIST LENT

As a kid, I thought beets tasted like dirt. As an adult, I still think they taste like dirt, but now that's what I like about them. In middle school, I was obsessed with the TV show *Blossom*, which is why I owned no less than ten different oversize floppy hats adorned with giant fake flowers. Today, I wouldn't be caught dead in a floppy sunflower hat, and the mere sight of Mayim Bialik (former *Blossom* star, on-again, off-again anti-vaxxer) makes me roll my eyes.

It's equal parts weird and surprising to look back on the person you once were and see how time has changed the way you see and think. For me, this change has been extremely apparent—and sometimes awkward—as I've grown more socially conscious and aware of how different types of people move through the world. For starters, being a feminist makes it difficult to listen to a good majority of music. I've given up on skipping songs with the word "bitch" in them, because that would deplete most of my iTunes library, but singing along to the top forty is a challenge. It's also hard to watch a lot of TV shows, and to sit silently in the theater as misogynistic movies you paid fifteen dollars to see play out across the screen. Sometimes it's hard to even have a simple conversation.

Growing up under patriarchy and white supremacy and

bigotry—which everyone does, since those are the systems that govern the world—means it can be hard to resist the less-than-obvious ways those forces creep into our speech, behavior, and superhero movies. Attempting to live a socially conscious life is a lot of work. As you become aware of all the ways our society is set up to put down marginalized people, from huge things like the prison system to small things like the words we use every day, you'll start seeing the world through completely new eyes.

At first, none of it will feel very fun. Actually, it never really feels very fun. Things you *want* to enjoy are ruined when you can recognize the not-so-subtle nasty messages they contain about women, LGBTQ folks, and people of color. And every day there seems to be a new word or phrase that has harmful origins or an underlying meaning you never thought about before. Sometimes it feels like no matter how hard I try, I can't say anything without offending someone. And since I'm a person who loves to run her mouth, that can be pretty difficult.

But I still try, even though from time to time I get it wrong. I've found that the best way to avoid hurting others is to steer clear of endorsing, watching, listening to, or participating in media or conversations that exclude or harm marginalized people. The best way to do that is to make a mental list, or at least have firm policies on what you will and won't stand for. I call this "Activist Lent," but instead of forty days, you give these things up for the rest of your life. A more accurate description might be "Activist Recently Discovered Severe Gluten Allergy," but that doesn't have a very good ring to it. Here are just a few of the games, habits, performing artists, and expressions I've given up in recent years—or at least believe I should have given up in recent years, even if I can't quite bring myself to cut the cord just yet.

GAME OF THRONES

This is many a feminist's guilty pleasure. The folks at HBO manage to lure so many of us back, even after giving us eighteen-month breaks between seasons to muster the will to quit. When my personal attempts to stop watching failed, I tried to turn off my feminist brain and just enjoy it; I've never managed that, either. Instead, I brace myself every time Tyrion enters a brothel, and complain about each episode for days after it airs. I'm hardly the first person to point this out, but despite being a badass, Khaleesi is a textbook white savior figure, with her glowing platinum hair and her posse of minions, all of whom are brown and constantly fawn over her. (I think I gasped during the scene when she crowd-surfed across a sea of brown nonspeaking extras as she celebrated her reign as their queen.) There's also the terrible story line of her relationship with Khal Drogo—he rapes her after taking her as a child bride, and then she falls in love with him; to add insult to injury, the actor who plays Khal Drogo publicly joked that being able to "rape beautiful women" was one of the perks of his role. He's since apologized, but as more and more actresses come forward about sexual assault in Hollywood, I can't help but wonder if this impulse explains rape as a plot device in too many films and television shows.

I digress. *Game of Thrones* is also mercilessly violent, and as a severe empath I'm often reduced to squealing and covering my eyes when gruesome death seems imminent. I can say pretty confidently that I feel angry with the show more than I like it. Nevertheless, I'm going to stick with it till the likely bitter end. Janet Mock calls this being a "critical fan"—I'm not going to give it up, but I don't gloss over the issues just because I enjoy immersing myself in the action. When people say they don't watch it, I respect that.

So why do I keep tuning in? For all the guilt I feel, there's no denying that it's an incredible show. It's one of the few that are truly unpredictable. Every time you like someone, they get killed off. (Though I pray Arya never sees this fate. I worry they're waiting for the series finale so it'll be too late for me to boycott the show in protest, like I did with *The Walking Dead*. RIP Glen.) I absolutely love the costumes, and since everyone and their brother watches the show, I enjoy participating in the collective water-cooler conversation it inspires. (Twitter is my water cooler.) But above all, I think what I find compelling about it is that, although the show is rife with horrible people with evil motives, they often get their comeuppance. We live in a world where too often bad people never see consequences. It's almost a relief to spend an hour each week in a place where they do.

THE SONG "BLIND MAN" BY XAVIER OMÄR

This song is something of a deep cut. If you're not a fan of neo-soul or Afrofuturistic bops, chances are you've never heard Xavier Omär's "Blind Man," but I can assure you it's quite a smooth jam, despite the cringey lyrics.

On first listen, when you're sort of half paying attention and can make out only a third of the words, it sounds like it's presenting a feminist message. "I can love you with my eyes closed / I don't lose sight of your beauty / 'Cause your heart is fine gold, baby / Imma take my time with your mind," Xavier croons. He praises his girl's ambition, her dreams, and her heart. While most men may just focus on this woman's "body like a queen," he suggests, he is no sexist—he cares about her mind.

But then we get into a dicey situation with some metaphors: "A blind man could love you just for who you are / Got 20/20 vision and I still don't see ya flaws / I said you make me feel good, and you ain't even touch me."

Is he saying his girl is so *physically* beautiful that a blind man could sense her beauty? Or is he saying that her inner beauty is strong enough that a blind person, who he believes would not care about physical appearance and therefore must be a connoisseur of inner beauty, would love her? The line "A blind man could love you just for who you are" suggests that a blind man somehow has more reason to judge a woman's inner beauty—I guess because Xav thinks her physical beauty wouldn't be able to make up for a bad personality? He tops it all off with a throwaway line that vaguely suggests blind people have to touch things a lot.

This doesn't make much sense, but what meaning we can get from it is offensive. For one thing, tons of blind people are in happy relationships with people they love and think are attractive; the suggestion that blind people are somehow more discerning when judging personalities is bizarre and othering. Remember the second line of the song, too: "I don't lose sight of your beauty"—a pretty sleazy pun that takes a cheap shot at blindness, especially when you consider that Xavier later insensitively brags about having twenty-twenty vision.

From a feminist perspective, Xavier's insistence on inner beauty—which we can only assume he's discussing because his girl is superhot in the first place—veers dangerously close to some lines in Drake's "Best I Ever Had": "Sweatpants, hair tied, chillin' with no makeup on / That's when you're the prettiest / I hope that you don't take it wrong." Drake, I do take it wrong, because sometimes I like to wear makeup, and I don't appreciate your ranking my styling choices because that's only going to make me self-conscious when I do decide to break out the MAC Ruby Woo. Though I don't forbid myself to listen to Drake, I do have him on notice for using that sensitive Auto-Tune to trick you into thinking his songs aren't all about policing women. "You're a good girl and you know it"—so what if I am?

R. KELLY

One of the hardest things to cut out of your life is a musical artist you like. You can be doing well, and then your favorite jam from 1997 comes on. You learned to love it before you understood the lyrics, back in that carefree time of your life when you thought you could get pregnant by sitting on a boy's lap. You might pause and wonder, "Maybe it's not so bad?" and enjoy the rest of the song uncomfortably before forgetting about it.

To this day I shudder to think of the middle school dances where my girlfriends and I belted out the lyrics to "Too Close" by Next, which I now know is a song about a guy having a boner on the dance floor and warning his dance partner she might feel it if she gets too close. Of course, erections are totally natural, and it's kinda nice that the fellas of Next felt it was important to disclose what was happening, even if they couldn't be more discreet than "You're making it hard for me."

This is not the case with R. Kelly, who has been accused of statutory rape, illegal marriage to a minor (Aaliyah), and, most recently, of brainwashing and holding women captive in a "sex cult." He's already profited off his music—there's nothing we can do about that. But we can refuse to play it, which I do. Not long ago, I was hanging out with my neighbors when they put on "Bump N' Grind." I hated to be the Debbie Downer, but I did it anyway. "I'm sorry, but you have to change this song. I don't see how you can listen to 'My mind's telling me no / But my body, my body's telling me yes' and not think, *Child predator*." My friends were understanding, but at first they tried to fight it. "But it's such a good song!" they cried, half dancing along as they objected.

I had to be firm. These were not questionable lyrics about "good girls"—R. Kelly is permanently and irrevocably tainted. "Fuck this guy," I said. "We will not pass go, we will not step in the name of love, we will not go to the hotel lobby, we will not take it to our rooms and freak somebody. We will stay right here and choose to listen to some other R&B singing sensation." And that is what we did.

CARDS AGAINST HUMANITY

I must confess: I have experienced this purposefully offensive game firsthand. But I promise, I only played it once, and I can truly say I will never do it again. I didn't know what it was when my friend, with a naughty twinkle in her eye, brought it out, and I felt like I was going to have a heart attack the entire time we played. If you're not familiar with Cards Against Humanity, its official tagline is "a party game for horrible people." It's basically group Mad Libs: Each player gets ten cards with words and phrases on them. The words and phrases range from questionable to terrible, and almost all of them have the potential to hit someone where it hurts. Here's a random selection of cards: *African children*, *The gays*, *An oversized lollipop*, *Court-ordered rehab*, and *Vehicular manslaughter*. If you're thinking these all sound like caricatures of what's considered "politically incorrect," it's because I made it a point just now to leave out any that were truly upsetting. Trust me, they're in there.

After everyone has been dealt their hand, you have to put your cards together in the middle to make a sentence based on a fill-in-the-blank prompt. The "Card Czar" picks the funniest—or most horrible—one, and the person who submitted it gets a point. It goes on this way until the most consistently offensive person is declared the winner. While I love a good game night, that evening felt like a *Game of Thrones*–style torture session. Instead of giving up, I tried my best to play along while sticking to my morals. This proved harder than expected; I lost a few rounds by playing it extra safe. But then I was able to turn it around. Maybe it was because I spend all day battling trolls, so I have perspective on how the worst minds of humanity work. Maybe it was that I wanted to get it over with. Maybe it was just beginner's luck. Maybe, deep down, I am a horrible person. Regardless, my friends said they were going to tell everyone, so I'm coming clean here: Somehow, some way, I won my first and last game of Cards Against Humanity.

RAP SONGS WITH TRUMP SHOUT-OUTS

I was one of the millions of American citizens who weren't prepared for the results of the 2016 presidential election. But one surprising consequence was realizing just how many of my favorite gym tunes name-checked Donald Trump, and I'm not talking about the recent classic "FDT (Fuck Donald Trump)" by YG. Nay, all throughout the 1990s and 2000s, rappers were shouting out Trump and his hotels as if they were symbols of prestige and wealth rather than tacky products of craven exploitation. I'll admit that I haven't purged these songs from my phone, but I stage a mini silent protest for choice lines such as...

"FLAWLESS (REMIX)," BEYONCÉ FEATURING NICKI MINAJ

I told him, "Meet me at the Trump, Ivanka."

"I WANNA BE WITH YOU," DJ KHALED

At the Trump, you bitches at the Radisson.

"DONALD TRUMP," MAC MILLER

Take over the world when I'm on my Donald Trump shit.

"WHAT MORE CAN I SAY," JAY-Z

I'm at the Trump International, ask for me.

"COUNTRY GRAMMAR (HOT SHIT)," NELLY

Bill Gates, Donald Trump, let me in now.

"IT'S GOIN' DOWN," YUNG JOC

Boys from the hood call me black Donald Trump.

THE FOLLOWING WORDS AND SAYINGS

There's an idea commonly thrown around conservative spaces that liberals, by objecting to certain words or phrases, want to censor free speech. An extreme example of this is the N-word: Every time a celebrity—or YouTube's most subscribed gamer—is caught saying it, the conversation is dominated by the idea that "It's not fair that you can say certain things and I can't." It should go without saying that anyone who wishes to say the N-word certainly *can*, but the reception and social consequences will differ based on whether or not you're black.

Regardless of how you feel about the word, the idea of words changing meaning between groups or individuals isn't a new concept, or one exclusive to black people. For example, my husband calls me "baby," and I usually respond with something like, "Aw. You still have to clean the bathroom." Meanwhile, if a dude on the corner calls me "baby," I'm going to roll my eyes. Words are like chameleons that way.

What these "Why are you censoring me?" people misunderstand is that no one is *forcing* anyone to change the way they speak. You can say anything you want; you won't face legal action for calling someone the N-word. But it doesn't mean you can say it free of consequences. You can totally start your company emails to your boss with "Dear ugly bitch"—you'll just get fired for it. By committing to march down the path of "political incorrectness," you're saying you're willing to sacrifice relationships with anyone who finds your language unacceptable.

Obviously, I'm not walking around calling my bosses—or anyone—ugly bitches. But beyond egregiously hurtful language, there are tons of other words and phrases that exclude, upset, or otherwise offend marginalized people that still find their way into everyday conversation. I try to eliminate these terms from my speech to be more conscious and welcoming, both to strangers and to people I know. With some of these, I had to be called out for using them before I understood how messed up they were; they've become so ingrained in our conversation that most of us don't even think about them. There's nothing wrong with that; we all have to learn somehow. The key is to avoid getting defensive, to listen to what people are telling you, and to work to do better. There are countless ways to express an idea—why would you want to use one that insults an entire group of people?

G*pped—I've definitely dropped this in a video without even thinking twice about it. It's such a colloquial, almost jokingly old-fashioned phrase that I was shocked when I learned its origins. So-called Gypsies—the historically nomadic ethnic group more appropriately known as Romani or Roma people—deal with horrific discrimination and oppression all over the world, and particularly in Europe, where certain businesses may still hang signs that read *No Gypsies*. Few companies will employ Roma people, so they are forced to beg, or worse, for money. They have been persecuted for centuries, at times forced into slavery, assimilation, and repatriation to their "countries of origin"; they have been treated as scapegoats for epidemics of disease and blamed for rising crime rates in several countries. Estimates of the number of Romani people killed during the Holocaust range from 200,000 to more than a million.

Today people use "g*pped" to suggest they've been swindled, which perpetuates the misconception that Romani people are untrustworthy or criminal. Saying your aunt "g*pped" you on sweet potatoes at Thanksgiving is not acceptable, and I was happy someone called me out on it. And while Free People and any number of other fashion labels push "Gypsy" wear for music festivals, the word is still a slur in many parts of the world. Which is why I avoid it even when it's meant to represent something positive, like overpriced crop tops.

"Hey, guys!"—Unless you find yourself in a group comprised exclusively of male-identifying people, there's a better word than "guys." For years, I began all my videos with a peppy "Hey, guys!" until someone gently pointed out that there's a more inclusive way to welcome my audience. Not every woman, female-identifying person, or nonbinary person feels uncomfortable with "guys"—I personally don't mind if someone uses "guys" when I'm in mixed company. But I still switched to "Hey, friends!" or "Hey, party people!" because some people do feel uneasy about "guys."

When I explain this concept to people, they're often incensed. "Ugh, you're so sensitive!" they cry. "I'm a woman and I don't care, so why should anyone else?" But I'd argue that these people are actually the sensitive ones, because instead of switching one word, they throw a temper tantrum.

"I feel fat"—The Facebook memory feature, which pulls past posts you made on the same date in previous years, is equal parts nostalgia and embarrassment. For me, in addition to photos of old friends I've lost touch with and excited praise for the *Sex in the City* movie, I was shocked to see how much I used to post about "feeling" or being fat.

"Bloated" is a feeling. "My stomach hates me because I ate an entire pizza" is a feeling. But "fat" is not a feeling. Everyone, no matter their size, has phases when they don't feel the best about their body, but associating those negative feelings with fat people increases the already huge stigma they face, from the misconception that being fat means you can't be healthy to the idea that it means you're dirty or unattractive. People feel so comfortable saying horrible things about fat people, it's almost as if weight were some kind of moral issue.

Statements like this also promote disordered eating, creating a tangled web of shame that touches the lives of so many people, regardless of their size. When I was younger, it seemed as if my mother was always on a diet, which meant I was always on a diet. When she eliminated carbs, I did, too; I drank SlimFast for breakfast and lunch even though it upset my stomach; I did my best to follow the makeshift Atkins diet by avoiding the foods on the list hanging on our fridge. I subscribed to the unfortunately common idea that being fat, or, really, anything other than thin, was the worst thing you could be, and that's where statements like "I'm so fat today" were coming from—a fear of becoming what I had been led to believe was a fate worse than drinking gritty "French Vanilla"–flavored "milkshakes" for two meals a day for the rest of my life.

When I got to acting school, disordered eating felt like the norm, if not actively encouraged. I would work out three times a day and limit myself to canned tuna and protein shakes. If anyone questioned whether I might have a problem, I responded with "Of course not! I'm eating!" At least one girl in my class of thirty acting students was hospitalized for her eating disorder, as were a few others, but it was never discussed. Instead, we treated it as a necessary consequence of looking "our best" for roles.

Since then, I've let go of the idea that one type of body is happy or healthy, and I've learned that the urge to put myself down about my weight is a direct consequence of the unrealistic beauty standards society has for women. And my impulse to acknowledge—or even apologize for—"feeling fat" has side effects that go far beyond my own self-esteem, too. It promotes bigoted attitudes toward fat people, from concern trolling ("I'm just worried about your health") to outright discrimination. When I worked at Anthropologie—not a store known for its inclusive range of clothes—racial profiling wasn't the only issue. Our loss-prevention team would flag customers over size 18 as potential shoplifters, because why else would they be there? Never mind that we sold shoes, home goods, and jewelry, which customers of any size could enjoy. And while I've had my own encounters with strangers who refuse to mind their business, I was shocked when one of my friends shared that random people will often congratulate her for ordering a salad because they assume someone of her size must be dieting.

From wearing crop tops or indulging in a sweet snack to having an active sex life, people have all sorts of warped and outdated ideas about what people with larger bodies should and shouldn't do with those bodies. This kind of thinking is invasive and rude, and it needs to stop. People of all sizes are happy with the way they look, and they don't feel like their size or shape is a bad thing. It's none of anyone else's business either way.

"I wanna kill myself"—There's something about the current political situation that makes it particularly easy to drop this into casual conversation. Trump has caused many of us to feel like we're constantly on the brink. But we're not.

I stopped saying this after a close friend lost a family member to suicide. I had accidentally erased my camera's memory card, losing a few hours' worth of work, and in a fit of frustration, I said, "Ugh, just fucking kill me!" My friend's immediate response was "Nothing is worth losing your life over. Please don't say that." I realized immediately how careless it was to suggest that death would be better than dealing with an inconvenience as inconsequential as a couple of lost files. You should always take it seriously if someone says they want to kill themselves. If everyone is always saying "I want to kill myself" when they really mean "I hate this situation" or "I would very much like to be excluded from this narrative," it becomes much more difficult to understand when people are serious and need help. Suicide is not a joke.

Lame—This is a hard one to quit, but pretty straightforward: The technical definition of "lame," according to *Merriam-Webster's Collegiate Dictionary*, is "having a body part and especially a limb so disabled as to impair freedom of movement." Since we apply it as a slang term to things that are ineffectual, insubstantial, boring, uncool, or otherwise bad, we imply that disabled people are ineffectual, insubstantial, boring, uncool, or otherwise bad. They're not.

Spaz—When I was in eighth grade, there was a girl in one of my acting classes who would slip into a mentally disabled character she called Sylvia. A group of us would be out somewhere, at the mall or a restaurant, and suddenly she would become Sylvia, fully embodying this character, and it would be our job to keep her from doing something too embarrassing or harmful. Thank goodness YouTube didn't exist in those days, because there would no doubt be ample video evidence of our horrendous shenanigans. Instead, you'll just have to believe me when I say everything from Sylvia's voice to her mannerisms was painful.

Once, we were in a drugstore, and she picked up a box of pads, went up to an employee, and asked, "Can I try these on?" Which of course sent us into a fit of giggles. (Think of the most obnoxious theater-kid stereotype you can dream up, and that was us, times ten.) The employee, not knowing what to say but not wanting to upset her, said, "Ummm...no...sorry...you can't." Sylvia, unperturbed, abandoned the interaction and knocked a row of adult diapers off a shelf in the next aisle, and we bolted out of the store.

Being kids, we were excited by the possibility of doing things

we weren't supposed to do, on top of "fooling" people into thinking someone had tasked a group of eighth graders with taking
care of a disabled child without an adult in sight. We thought
the whole thing was just hilarious, but I don't think I really need
to explain why it wasn't. For one thing, it was someone's job to
clean up our mess, and I'm sure some underpaid employee was
chewed out for letting us wreak havoc in the store. For another,
creating a spectacle of Sylvia made it seem okay to stereotype
or mock people with physical and mental challenges, people who
have a huge range of abilities. Just like saying someone is being
"retarded," calling someone a "spaz"—a derogatory term for people with "spastic paralysis," which is known as cerebral palsy
when it's congenital—ignores the prejudices and difficulties disabled people face, and instead turns them into a punchline.

Spirit animal—This is another phrase I was rightfully called out
for. It's not uncommon to hear people refer to everything from
their favorite actress to the latest viral meme as their "spirit animal." It's meant as a term of endearment, so what could be wrong
about that?

Until the American Indian Religious Freedom Act of 1978,
Native Americans were often prevented—sometimes violently—
from accessing sacred sites, keeping ceremonial items that were
illegal under U.S. law (such as eagle bones or peyote), and performing ceremonies or rituals without gawking onlookers or
questioning from authorities. Keeping this in mind, "spirit animal" is actually a gross oversimplification of an important part
of a culture that has long been actively oppressed, stifled, and
ignored in racial justice discourse.

The ways that indigenous people have been forced into assimilation are so specific: They were moved off sacred lands, their
names were changed, and their languages were purged so
aggressively that colonizers would destroy cultural and religious

artifacts that featured words. The message was clear: If you want to stay in this country, you have to be like us. So it probably hurts when non-Native people talk about cartoon characters and rainbow bagels as being their "spirit animals." (Meanwhile, we live in a country where people, including the president, flip their shit when people say "happy holidays" instead of "merry Christmas.") "Spirit animal" is not an appropriate metaphor to explain that you identify with the snarky cat from *Sabrina the Teenage Witch*.

<u>**"That's so crazy!"**</u>—A whole cache of mental-health terms have migrated into casual use. Some act as slurs—such as "psycho" or "psychopath"—and others are things we might say to lightly make fun of ourselves: "Oh, I'm just so OCD about my bathroom!" Often, these words are used to explain away systemic racism, bigotry, and murder; any time a white man opens fire on a school, or a movie theater, or a concert, people, trying to understand the tragedy, say, "He must have been crazy." The effect of this is twofold: People who have mental illnesses may feel ashamed to seek help, and the systemic problems at the root of the actions (lax gun-control laws, toxic masculinity, etc.) continue to go unacknowledged.

Mental health is so stigmatized that we barely talk about the original issues we're dealing with, much less about how it hurts when friends use "insane" to describe the objectively awful political situation. Not to mention the fact that labeling violent or bigoted people as "crazy" or "mentally ill" perpetuates two harmful ideas: that mentally ill people are dangerous, and that bigotry is something people can't control. I admit that I never even thought about how often I deemed the news "crazy" until someone called me out for it on Twitter. I still slip up now and then, but I try to replace "crazy/insane" with "wild" or "unbelievable"—it conveys exactly the same sense, without the harm.

〰〰〰〰〰

I could go on, but don't worry—I won't go into the movie portion of my list, which would no doubt ruin any future Netflix and chill plans. It can feel like a lot to keep track of, I know, but once you get used to this kind of self-editing, it can be kind of fun. You're helping to make the world a better place for marginalized people, and by holding yourself accountable in everyday situations, you're also teaching by example. You know how, when you were a kid, you used to put all the pillows on the floor and hop from one to the other because if you touched the carpet it was lava? Think of your Activist Lent list as the lava. Just make sure to apologize gracefully if you fall in.

CHAPTER TEN

UNFRIENDED

Ending a friendship used to be simple. Like when your best friend moved to Boston to live with her dad and stepmom, leaving you high and dry in South Florida. Bam. Friendship over. Sure, you breathlessly promised to KIT (keep in touch) and LYLAS (love ya like a sister), but you had no interest in *actually* going to Boston because you imagined it resembled a town in Siberia where all the men wore Patriots jerseys and used "wicked" to mean the opposite of what it's supposed to mean. Or like in sixth grade, after your girlfriend confided in you that she'd gotten her first period, and you made a cheap Red Sea joke in geography class and she never forgave you. Even if you regretted it later, the friendship breakup was cut-and-dried: There was a clear cause and effect that both parties understood. Obviously you were just jealous, but that didn't erase the hurt or embarrassment. (Those were the days, right? When middle school girls longed for their periods, not in the "But seriously, where the fuck is my period?!" sort of way, but more of an "I can't wait to run through a field dressed in all white celebrating my womanhood!!!" kind of thing.) In the end, you were persona non grata at your former friend's coed pool party, but at least you knew where you stood.

Today, Facebook is where friendships go to die. If you're some-how one of the last people left on earth who is not on Facebook, you are both worthy of envious admiration and hella suspect. How do you remember the birthdays of random people you interned with in college? How do you keep track of how often your mother-in-law plays—and CRUSHES—*Bejeweled*? What about the bloody C-section photos of women you can't quite place because they've changed their last names and their profile photos are pictures of babies playing with puppies? Seriously, who the hell is that woman, and what did I do to deserve her afterbirth in my Facebook feed?

Despite the wealth of information Facebook abstainers miss out on, they're also spared the gut-wrenching feeling that comes when you realize someone you once considered a friend believes America should be celebrating "White History Month." It should be as simple as it was in sixth grade: Friendship over. Though the process seems easy—you literally just have to click a button to officially unfriend someone—it dredges up all kinds of difficult questions. The abandoned friend may have no idea what she did to deserve being purged from your timeline, and you may have no interest in dealing with her long enough to tell her. It couldn't have been the "Leave Ivanka Alone!" meme she posted at two thirty in the morning, could it? Are political differences really enough to destroy a friendship that may have survived multiple moves, fights, betrayals, and drunken confessions of "I knew that dress you wore to prom ten years ago looked bad but I didn't say anything"? The fact that you never have to see each other in person to hash it out means you can forget about closure.

Someone once told me that, for black folks, being friends with white people is like holding a bomb and not knowing when it'll go off. While there's probably some truth to this analogy, I've found that everyone, no matter their race, gender, sexuality, or number of pro-choice buttons on their organic hemp grocery bags, has the capacity to blow up on Facebook, leaving everyone they know confused and covered in shards of incoherent ramblings.

"Blowing up" doesn't just mean spoiling the latest episode of *The Walking Dead*. (Though that falls under the General Asshole category and should also be avoided, unless you want me to give you the ice-queen eyebrow next time we see each other at a party. Also, why are you still watching *The Walking Dead*?) No, what I'm talking about are the people who choose to use their status updates to uphold systems of oppression, perpetuating misinformation, intolerance, prejudice, and, ultimately, white supremacy. That's kind of high-minded language to describe your high school guidance counselor's misspelled rants about illegal immigration, I know, but white supremacy works on every level, from the White House (duh) to your uncle Ron. And this is one of the few times I'm comfortable using the phrase "not just white people"—too many of my skinfolk are all too happy to suck on the teat of the white sup. If you've ever caught Milwaukee sheriff David Clarke doing one of his Fox News appearances—though I don't know why you'd have that on—you know what I mean.

Combine this layer cake of white supremacy expression with the ways social media turns us all into lab rats, trained to expect praise and attention every time we so much as comment on Jennifer Lopez's hair, and it's no wonder Facebook forces you to reckon with every single one of your relationships. Where else can your mom, mailman, boss, and Tinder date all hang out and shoot the shit, together? And they aren't talking about the weather. I'm not going to say that Facebook brings out the absolute worst in people—that honor goes to Sunday afternoon at Trader Joe's—but it does encourage people to be petty, competitive, arrogant, and gossipy, and to engage in WWE-style dramatics. Except this arena has no rules, referee, or ejection policy.

Which brings us back to friendship breakups. Sometimes you may want to forget you ever met these people (okay, maybe not your mom). As everyone knows, these days the first step to forgetting you ever met someone is purging them from your social media accounts. But how do you determine when a friendship can—or should—be mended and when it's time to pull the plug?

Like your relationship status at age seventeen, it's complicated.

It's not possible for two people to agree on everything, no matter how well they get along. Hell, my husband and I have an argument almost every time we have to pick a movie to watch. (He always wants a gory horror flick; I'm more of an action/thriller type.) But those are the type of agree-to-disagree moments every relationship is made of.

Politics is a different story. You may have passionate debates with your die-hard liberal friend who posts selfies in a #StillWithHer T-shirt, but you know at the end of the day the two of you are on the same team. But when it comes to basic human rights issues—like trans bathroom laws, affordable health care, or same-sex marriage—agreeing to disagree feels nearly impossible. An opinion stops being "just an opinion" when it supports the mistreatment or oppression of others, which is why political differences can tear families apart and *Troll II* can't. This quote from @SonofBaldwin, also known as the writer Robert Jones Jr., says it best: "We can disagree and still love each other unless your disagreement is rooted in my oppression and denial of my humanity and right to exist."

꙼꙼꙼꙼

So let's say one of your Facebook friends has crossed the line and posted a disgusting meme slut-shaming Melania Trump for taking nude photos back in the day. You're at a crossroads. Are you mad at this Facebook friend for slut-shaming a grown woman who can do whatever the hell she wants with her body? Or are you mad at her for making you defend a woman whose husband and politics are absolutely reprehensible (but who can still do whatever the hell she wants with her body)? For the purposes of this analogy, let's say it's both. Which, coincidentally, is the correct answer. What do you do? Leave a lengthy comment about bodily autonomy? Reply with an eye-roll GIF that's completely open to interpretation? (Are you rolling your eyes at the post, or at Melania's totally consensual adult nudes?) Or do you pull out the big guns and unfriend altogether?

Relationships aren't exactly "ride or die," no matter how many pinkie promises or drunken declarations one might make—and that's where this gets tricky. For some friends, acquaintances, or coworkers, it may be easier for everyone if you silently end the virtual friendship instead of trying to reason with them in the comments. For others, unfriending will just make everything worse.

To help you figure out if it's worth it to delete and never look back, I've made a handy guide, outlining all the relationships you may have on Facebook and the potential drama they have bottled up inside them, waiting to destroy your Thanksgiving.

In case you're wondering, no, the little icons are not Iron Man helmets—they're supposed to be old-school sad drama masks. But I suspect Iron Man would also hate stirring up unnecessary Facebook drama, so whatever the icons evoke for you is okay with me. Remember that in a past life I was a graphic designer.

OH, THE "FRIENDS" YOU'LL UNFRIEND

Family

Ideally, we'd never be forced to accept our family members as friends on social media in the first place. Though you might appreciate being tagged in weekly ~*~SHARE THIS IF YOU LOVE

YOUR BEAUTIFUL, PERFECT DAUGHTER~*~ posts, your life is probably not improved by knowing that your great-aunt has discovered anti-abortion memes. (Even if you would like to know how the hell she found that website—the last you heard, she still used dial-up.) And you don't necessarily want the whole gang to see what you're posting, either.

But sometimes denying or ignoring a family member's friend request—or going the full distance and unfriending them altogether—is just asking for trouble when a cousin's wedding comes around. Not only that, but chances are they know where you live and have access to embarrassing photos of you from when you had braces and did a weird thing with your eyes whenever someone brought out a camera because you thought you'd mastered Tyra's "smizing" lesson on *America's Next Top Model*. Proceed with caution.

Current Classmates

While I've never been to prison, I've marathoned enough episodes of MSNBC's *Lockup* to realize that school is the closest most of us will ever come to the clink. (Unless you're like me and had to spend three hours in the juvenile assessment center for stealing tarot cards, but that's a different story.) Your school experience likely consisted of monotonous days spent trapped in an institutional facility for hours at a time with random people you wouldn't choose. Sentence: twelve to life.

What I'm saying is, tensions are already high. One of the best and worst things about Facebook is that it means you never have to look someone in the eye when you tell them they suck. But if you're unfriending someone you could easily run into in the cafeteria or dining hall on fish stick day, that aspect goes out the window—and the potential for in-person drama is huge.

Former Classmates

Ah, yes, the classic Facebook friend, the one everyone is talking about when they're like, "Suddenly everyone I know has two kids and is running an ugly yoga pants pyramid scheme out of their spare bedroom!" These are people you haven't seen in a few years—maybe more—but you have a good enough idea of who they are that you enjoy creeping through their profile, scrolling past eight hundred pics of their moderately cute children to see if they've somehow maintained their looks since high school. Ending these friendships is relatively low drama, unless you still live in the same small town you grew up in, or plan on going to your high school or college reunion (which, unless it has an open bar, you can probably skip). The only risk is the loss of old happy memories, which you've most likely embellished anyway.

I've had to drop the Facebook ax on far too many former class-mates over the years. One girl, whom I'll call Sophie, is particularly memorable. Sophie and I were never close in high school, but we had a few friends in common and hung out a handful of times. While perfectly pleasant, Sophie was far too wild for my tastes—your classic "poor little rich girl" who had more money than she knew what to do with, so she spent it on drugs and getting her light blue vintage Mercedes detailed every weekend. Seriously—no one needs their car cleaned that often.

Given Sophie's party-girl past, I was surprised to discover that just six years after we graduated, she'd transformed into an evan-gelical conspiracy theorist. She filled my Facebook feed with a stream of obnoxious anti-vaxxer memes, Bible quotes, and rants against birth control. Well, maybe not that surprising—Catholic guilt is fucked up and real. While most of her posts were beyond eye-roll inducing, I kept her around for the "I can't believe this is who she turned into" factor. Don't judge—you know you've got more than a few of those in your feed right now.

But Sophie made a swift exit from my virtual circle in November 2008, right after Obama won the presidential election. While most of my friends were celebrating, Sophie was having a full-blown meltdown. She announced that she and her husband would be making some staffing changes to their family business in honor of Obama's win. Something like: "We're going to stroll through the parking lot, and anyone who has an Obama sticker on their bumper will be let go. Let's see if this was the 'change' they were hoping for." No. Just no.

I should've pulled the plug on our internet pseudo-friendship right then and there, but instead I did what I almost always advise people *not to do*: hopped into the comments to "remind" Sophie that it's super illegal to fire someone because of who they voted for. I tried my best to reason with her, but she wasn't having it. After she made a few thinly veiled racist comments about welfare and compared Obama to Hitler, I decided I'd had enough and happily hit the *Block* button on our relationship.

After the 2016 election went the way it did, a lot of people were saying this kind of unfriending was bad, that liberals were living in internet echo chambers separated from the concerns of "the rest of the country." While I do think it's our responsibility to educate people in our own communities, you can't build bridges with someone who not only refuses to do the work but also fires anyone who might be willing to. If we stopped to have an educational conversation with every offensive or hurtful person we've ever met, it would consume our entire lives. As much as it sucks, Sophie's own bias was going to keep her from being receptive to what I, a black person she hung out with three times in 2000, was telling her.

The lesson here is that ironic online friending is tacky, so when it blows up in your face, admit you brought this particular bigot on yourself and unfriend ASAP.

Coworkers

Take it from someone who's made this mistake too many times to count: Skip the inevitable drama by not friending or following coworkers online until you or they have quit. Similar to prison/school, these are people you're forced to interact with every day—they're not your real friends until they earn it.[*] Coworkers are best seen as undercover agents, able to turn on you at any moment and use your gossip—and Facebook posts—against you.

Besides, any potential friending that happens while you work together could bring drama to the office, and office drama has the potential to morph into financial drama, as in your ass could end up fired.[†] When it comes to work and social media, it's best to heed that immortal reality show mantra: "I'm not here to make friends."

(If it's too late and you already friended a coworker who turned out to be an irredeemable jerk on Facebook, check your profile settings and make sure they're on limited profile so they don't have access to your drunken photos and embarrassing status updates.)

---

[*] Real coworker friendship requires repeated IRL hangouts that don't involve conversations about work or former coworkers.
[†] And you definitely don't want to connect on social media with the person who could fire you, so do not friend your boss.

Exes/People You've Slept With

Unless you're one of those freaks who can legitimately stay friends with your ex, keeping people you've dated or slept with in your digital feed is just nosy, and probably not good for your mental health. Lucky for you, these people are easy to unfriend: As soon as they say something even remotely awful, or the moment you get sick of their excessive new boo-thang PDA, you have valid reason to say peace. After all, if you wanted to tolerate that, you wouldn't have dumped them in your car in the Dairy Queen parking lot. (Though I hope you had the courtesy to drive them home afterward.)

Then there are the "I can't believe I slept with you, what are you even doing here?" moments. In college, I occasionally hooked up with an RA. He was my first semireal relationship, meaning sometimes we'd go out to dinner before ending up in his dorm room. He was handsome and funny enough that I over-looked some of his annoying qualities, including his insistence that my middle-class upbringing wasn't a "real black experience" in comparison to his rough Detroit childhood. Or how he'd tease me about the high-pitched squealing I was known to partake in whenever I hung out with my best friend, De'Lon. Since the RA and I kept things casual, there were no hurt feelings when things fizzled out, securing his spot in my feed and in the fuzzy part of my memory reserved for nostalgia about carefree youth. But one comment changed all that.

After I posted a photo of me and De'Lon drunkenly cud-dled up at a piano bar on De'Lon's birthday, my RA fling casu-ally commented, "I knew he wasn't gay." Like a caramel bacon jalapeño cookie that leaves you thinking, *Here's a combination of things I'd never put together*, this guy managed to cram homopho-bia, slut-shaming, and jealousy into one tiny bite-size sentence.

And he was happy to say it publicly, on the record! In what universe is that your business, guy-I-used-to-get-naked-with-but-don't-anymore? What I should've done was tell him to take his outdated notions of masculinity and sexuality and place them directly in his heterosexual anal sphincter, but instead I just ended our online friendship and texted De'Lon a big LOL. We are still besties, and he is still very gay.

IRL Friends

Mayday, mayday! Major drama alert! For our purposes, I'm defining IRL friends as people you text regularly and go out of your way to fit into your offline life. If you live in New York, this may only happen, like, once a month, but that once a month is cherished. These are people you have no business communicating with on Facebook because they're sitting across from you at brunch and that's rude as hell. Unfriending them could affect your entire circle and make hangouts really uncomfortable. Your other friends may have to *choose between you*, which is so high school.

If you're seriously contemplating virtually ditching a real-life friend, you should consider talking privately, away from your Facebook audience, first. If possible, take the conversation offline entirely and chat in person or by phone; if not, email is infinitely better than Facebook chat. Maybe whatever they said that enraged you got lost in translation, and there's an opportunity for personal growth that one or both of you need.

But no matter how close you and the other person may be, even if you go into it with the gentlest and most understanding of mind-sets, it doesn't always work out. In 2013, after George Zimmerman was acquitted for the murder of Trayvon Martin, the last thing I expected was to get into a Facebook argument with one of my childhood friends—let's call him Andy—over whether my grief was valid. Although we'd known each other since we were kids, Andy and I couldn't have been raised in more different environments. The oldest of three boys, he is white and grew up in a trailer park with his mom and alcoholic stepdad. My parents were divorced, and my mom and I lived in a three-bedroom house just across the canal from Andy's trailer.

We were close friends. Though I was only a year and a half older, Andy began calling me his big sister during my sophomore year of high school. He would tell me about the girls he was interested in, and I would give him advice if I approved or a side eye when I didn't. The single time I was ever grounded, he happily snuck into my backyard so we could share a joint through my bedroom window.

Our friendship was so obviously platonic, my super-conservative mother didn't even bat an eye when he showed up at our doorstep one night in tears looking for a place to stay. His stepfather had the kind of horrible temper that always seems to accompany a drinking habit, so Andy had stormed off, vowing to never go back. He slept in our guest room that night, and I promised he could stay as long as he liked, even though I had no business offering.

If he sometimes saw me as a spoiled little rich girl with no problems, he never mentioned it, and I never detected it. He was always kind, and we treated each other with admiration and respect. So it was pretty surprising when, years later, despite the fun times we'd shared catching up over Christmas breaks and reliving old inside jokes on each other's Facebook walls, he jumped into one of my posts about our nation's broken justice system. He tried to shame me for ignoring "the overwhelming drug and gang violence that dwarfs 'vigilante, and police' shootings all over."

I had to take a deep breath. And then I began to type.

I should've taken the conversation offline. Instead, I replied to his comment. I was angry, I was sad, and I felt like he was willfully refusing to understand where I was coming from. I wrote that it's possible to care about more than one thing at a time and that it was rude to derail our conversation by suggesting there were "more important things to talk about." The entire thread descended into a silent screaming match as friends of every race and creed tried to explain to Andy why the idea that "racism is a distraction to divide us" was among the top three things people of color are sick of hearing from white people.

Andy hit all the defensive-white-guy classics. "The Irish were slaves, too!" "Classism is the real issue!" Sharing a Morgan Freeman meme about colorblindness! As we all know, if Morgan Freeman, professional spokesman for black people and voice of God, says we should "stop talking about race," then the argument is settled.

By this point, the thread had gotten out of control. Every time I tried to finish a thought, three new comments would pop up and the conversation would burrow deeper and deeper into the ground. There was no turning back. I sent Andy a private message to try to save him (and myself) further embarrassment. Though I thought he was totally misguided, I focused on the way he'd presented his ideas and not the ideas themselves. I said it was condescending for him to tell grown adults that they're "wasting" their time by talking about whatever they're interested in instead of whatever he's interested in. I added that, as challenging as his upbringing may have been, it didn't give him the right to speak over me, a black woman, as I discussed my experiences with racism and my fears about living in a world where my skin color is seen as a threat. In addition to the profoundly ignorant things he'd said, he'd been talking down to me, as if I were incapable of managing my time, interests, and emotions.

I ended my message by saying he didn't need to respond unless he was prepared to apologize. He sent back another Morgan Freeman meme. I clicked "unfriend."

Could the friendship have been salvaged if we'd talked over the phone? The fact that he thought a meme was the best way to respond tells me no, but who knows? People who seem like jerks online often just don't understand that their humor isn't carrying—that what they think is a lighthearted joke actually reads as dismissive and cocky.

At the very least, a phone call would've saved me the time and energy I spent hunched over my laptop, furiously typing and backspacing to try to mediate between Andy and my friends. The internet is a great place to be exposed to certain conversations, but a terrible place to have conversations yourself, especially if a friendship is on the line. Choose your opponents (and your friends, duh) wisely.

Internet Friends

Internet friends are people you've built a relationship with over a few months—or even years—but haven't actually met in person, or have met in person only a few times. While internet friendships are very legitimate relationships, they're usually a lot easier to end because people have this lingering idea that they aren't *real.* (*Homo sapiens* spent hundreds of thousands of years only interacting with each other face-to-face, and that whole "human history" thing is hard to shake, no matter how convenient ordering your dinner on an iPad is.) Plus, you don't risk running into internet friends at a party postbreakup, and you usually have few IRL friends in common, if any. (If this weren't true, you would probably see them more often!) It gets a little sticky if you're all in the same industry and do most of your work virtually, but even so, these kinds of connections are supposed to come and go. Don't lose sleep over it.

Randos

Oh, right, that guy. Who cares? These are people you probably shouldn't have linked up with online anyway, friends of friends of friends you meet at parties or the men who start talking to you about "synergy" at PR events and send you friend requests before you're in your Uber home. When they get out of line online, your first reaction is "Who?" You can't even remember where you met them or when you added them on Facebook.

Why did you add them in the first place? Maybe you thought they'd be a good business contact, or you liked a joke they made about airline food, and you imagined your friendship blossoming like cherry trees in the spring. This is the wrong attitude to have this late in the Facebook game. Hanging out with someone once is not enough to let them into your online circle. They can float in pending-request purgatory until you're confident they're worth the risk. They don't have to know you hit *Decline*. Maybe you're just so busy living an exciting and glamorous lifestyle that you forget to look at your Facebook friend requests. Odds are they'll quickly forget about you, too.

ᘉᘉᘉᘉᘉ

Now that we've laid out the types of Facebook fools who could potentially meet your ban hammer, I've created a handy flow-chart that will help you decide how to proceed when someone inevitably blows up your feed.

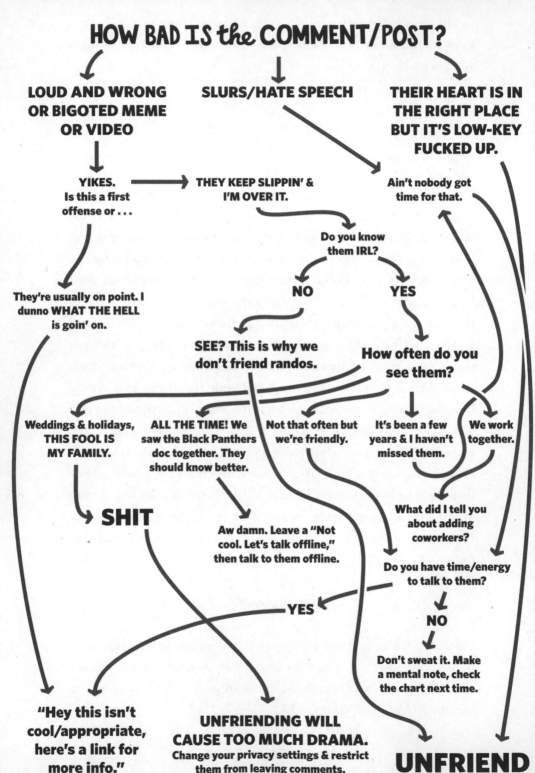

With all this drama lurking just beneath the *Comment* button, you may be wondering why you're still on Facebook anyway. Some people thrive on the attention, on the constant stream of new information and ideas and infuriating arguments and incredible links you have to click to believe. Some people make it work. But everyone's social media experience is different. As with any social network, you have to decide why you're on Facebook, and what you want or need to get out of it. Just as most serious conversations about race, gender, and politics are better had offline, there's nothing healthy about Facebook stalking, even though that's essentially what the platform was built for. If you find yourself feeling guilty because you didn't post enough photos of your recent trip to Bermuda, or if the unfriending experience has left you feeling gross and petty (and also like you have no friends, at all), it's possible you need to log off for a while.

I know this probably sounds a little hypocritical, coming from a former social media callout queen and oversharer. If I hadn't succumbed to my worst online tendencies, I probably wouldn't have my career, let alone a book deal. But even as I've made massive, viral mistakes, I've stuck with these platforms because I've seen the good things they have to offer. In addition to *loving* my friends' dog photos, I'm in a private Facebook group of WOC comedians from around the country, where we share audition horror stories and offer advice on everything from on-camera makeup to getting a better agent to dealing with difficult coworkers. It's really cathartic, and I've made some great connections and friends there that I doubt I would have offline. So for all the nuclear devastation that can take place on Facebook, the site isn't a completely hopeless disaster.

But as long as people have air in their lungs and Wi-Fi in their pockets, there will always be someone who makes you second-guess the access they have to your time and timeline. If worse comes to worst and you can't unfriend, well—do you think you could manage two accounts? Embrace your new identity, Helga von Schwenderlaufer.

CHAPTER ELEVEN

LAST NAME BASIS

I never thought I'd marry a white guy. I also never thought I wouldn't marry a white guy. In reality I never thought much about who I'd marry at all, because for a long time I was certain marriage wasn't for me. My parents' divorce made me skeptical of the whole institution, and the idea that I should decide in advance which races are acceptable for life partnership struck me as, well, superficial. Yet many people treat my relationship with Patrick, the man I've been with for eleven years (who just so happens to be white), like it's evidence that I'd been plotting some kind of racial coup. It's almost like I have to admit to having a white husband in the hushed tones I'd usually reserve for the confessional booth—too often, my followers discuss their shock/confusion/disappointment about the moment when they found out my husband was white. As if he were a terminal illness I'd been diagnosed with. (How do I know? Well, they have these conversations in my Instagram comments.)

Others assume Patrick's whiteness was the foundation on which we built our modest, two-bedroom relationship. If whiteness were the reason for my relationship with Patrick, I can assure you we would've broken up a long time ago. His race doesn't help when one of our dogs gets diarrhea all over the living room carpet; it sure as hell doesn't help when he destroys our bathroom or when I need to do my makeup but he's in there shaving. Patrick's whiteness doesn't take care of any of the demanding aspects of partnership. Like any relationship, ours requires work.

Our story is like something out of an early-2000s fairy tale: We met at a house party I'd gone to because I wanted to hook up with someone else—the guy who was throwing the party. It was around the holidays, and I hit it off with Pat because I assumed he was in a relationship. I'd never had a serious boyfriend before, having always kept relationships in that awesome purgatory stage when you insist, "We're NOT dating—we only hang out after eleven p.m.!" After the party—where I, fortunately, did not hook up with the host—Pat told one of our mutual friends he liked me, and she set up a "group date" at Panera Bread. Very casual. She never showed up, so we dined on bread bowls alone and then shared our first kiss in his car after I mocked the mistletoe hanging from his rearview mirror. We've been together ever since.

Today, he and I have a podcast—*Last Name Basis*, download it on iTunes!!!—so people are used to our dynamic: We make fun of each other, a lot, and talk a lot of shit. Pat's sense of humor was the first thing I noticed about him, and I loved that he didn't pull any punches when it came to razzing me. When we first moved to New York we bought a used Nintendo Wii off Craigslist, and our *Mario Kart* battles would get so intense that I worried the neighbors would call the cops; we competed with the out-of-work opera singer downstairs by screaming things like "You drive like a fucking retiree, and I am going to destroy you!"

Beautiful, right? Not everyone thinks so. The first time the internet gave me shit for my relationship with Patrick was when I decided to document our three-year (dating) anniversary on YouTube. I was twenty-six and getting really into making videos at the time; Patrick was waiting tables at Olive Garden to pay off his student loans. He didn't really get the YouTube thing, but he decided to go along with it anyway. I told him we could talk about how we met and that it would be really funny and adorable, but not so adorable that he'd come off as soft or uncool.

Back on our three-year anniversary, we weren't really a "public" couple, so when we made our YouTube debut, I'm sure more than a few people were shocked to see the nice girl with the hair tutorials trading slurred profanities with her white boyfriend. On top of drinking a lot of wine, I'd also lost my voice, so I sounded like a Russian gangster.

In the grand scheme of provocative #content, we were being tame. We made some off-color jokes about the fact that Pat had named his new black hatchback "the Black Fist," and we yelled at our dogs between sips of wine. But unlike my other posts, which were produced and planned, the video wasn't intended to be anything but a chance to be silly and mess around. As we drank more wine, we started play-fighting more, and the types of biting comments we always make started to flow. It was all in good fun. I didn't think too much about it when, the next day, I woke up with a headache and posted it.

Even back in 2009, when callout culture was but a twinkle in Twitter CEO @jack's eye, I was foolish to think this video wouldn't get noticed. The jokes were inappropriate, and I had a big enough following that a sizable number of people would see it. Still, I was surprised when I checked my email and saw an inbox full of enraged comments. They weren't even really about all the "not PC" things we were saying; instead, they were from a group of very disgruntled black viewers who believed interracial relationships were a plot to destroy the black family. Any black woman who would willingly date a white man, they assured me, must be pathologically self-hating.

The video quickly racked up fifty thousand views, more than anything I'd ever posted at that time. As I combed through the comments, I started to notice a trend: The most aggressive posts came from avatars and usernames that recalled ancient Egyptian and Afrocentric themes. Who were these people?

Apparently my video had been shared by a popular "hotep," which inspired a wave of commenters to attack me for "disrespecting my blackness." I soon learned that hotep (which is an Egyptian word that roughly means "to be at peace") was the name adopted by black folks across the internet as both an insult and an identity. Hoteps often dabble in misogyny, homophobia, conspiracy theories, and fanciful African origin stories that link eating red meat to white supremacy; feminism to a plot to destroy the black family; and everything from hurricanes and headaches to slavery. According to my new hotep "fans," I was so self-hating and superficial that I'd hopped into bed with the first white guy who would have me. And to make matters worse, he wasn't even a rich white guy!

This logic still confuses me to this day: It's superficial to date a white guy, but not superficial if you make sure he's got some money? The comments ranged from laughable—"I just think you should know: He's cheating on you. I can tell by his eyes"—to full-on misogynoir: "Black women are so desperate for white acceptance they'll be with a white guy for three years even though he hasn't put on a ring on it." I was so shocked by the intensity of the comments coming from black people in particular—and the fact that almost no one directed any of the vitriol at Pat—that I took the video down.

Then I got a text from a friend: "hey girl...just wanted to let you guys know I saw an ad for an interracial porn site and it was you and pat? hope ur ok xoxo." I didn't bother asking what my friend was searching for when they stumbled across the ad (no judgment) and instead requested a link, ASAP. Yes, someone had spliced up our drunk anniversary home video so that lines like "Are you nervous?" and "We've never made a video together before..." took on a completely different meaning. The still image was a shot of me and Pat drunkenly clinking our glasses and toasting to our foray into amateur erotica. Awesome. Thankfully I was able to file a claim through YouTube to get it removed before someone tried to add it to my IMDb page.

μΛΛΛΛΛΛΛΑΑ

Where did the idea that interracial relationships are incompatible with the fight for equality come from? My white husband doesn't make me any less black, or any less dedicated to the fight for racial justice—just as being married to a man doesn't make me any less of a feminist or passionate about women's issues. Perhaps some forget that interracial marriage was at one time, not so long ago, a civil rights issue; it was illegal in many states until 1967, when the landmark Supreme Court case *Loving v. Virginia* determined that anti-miscegenation laws* were unconstitutional. "There is patently no legitimate overriding purpose independent of invidious racial discrimination which justifies this classification," the court wrote in the *Loving* decision. "The fact that Virginia prohibits only interracial marriages involving white persons demonstrates that the racial classifications must stand on their own justification, as measures designed to maintain White Supremacy." In other words, the idea that white people should not "mix" with other races upholds white supremacy. It's segregation. It's racist.

To be fair, I can see why some people of color assume the worst when it comes to folks with white partners. Perhaps they've been fetishized, or dealt with more blatant racism, in an interracial relationship themselves. Or maybe they've met POC who wave their white partners around like a badge of honor, or who use

---

* Anti-miscegenation laws referred to interracial marriage, but they also extended beyond it; in Virginia, where *Loving* originated, interracial sex was also illegal.

their white partners to put down members of their own race. So it's no wonder they look at me and my white husband with one eyebrow raised. But the same frustration I feel when white people make assumptions about who I am because of my blackness is echoed when black people assume I must be a certain kind of person because my partner is white. It often feels as if the whole world is placing expectations on me and pressuring me to limit my experience—or to define it entirely—based on my race.

Needless to say, Pat didn't show up in another video of mine for years—I realized then that I didn't want to make my private life so public. But that hasn't stopped people from making bizarre assumptions about our relationship. Sometimes they're not so abusive, but they're no less rooted in racism. A few years ago I was at a conference when a black woman came up to me to commiserate about how much dating black men sucks. "So happy to meet you!" she said, breathlessly. "We have so much in common—my husband is white, too." (Note: This doesn't mean we have very much in common.) She continued: "I gotta commend you, girl—these niggas don't have their shit together. When I was single I said to myself, 'I need to get me a white man.'"

I was at the conference for work—acting as the spokeswoman for a family planning site that encouraged women to use birth control—so I tried to keep my jaw off the floor. Is this how people assumed I felt about my relationship? In my mind, I was screaming, *My dad is a black guy! The last dude I kinda-sorta dated was a black guy! My best friend is a black guy! I probably would've married him if he weren't gay, but that's not the point!* Instead, I told her I didn't go looking for any certain type of guy—Pat was just who I fell in love with—and flashed her an obviously fake smile as I thanked her for saying hello.

This should go without saying, but there's nothing inherently special, progressive, or earth-shattering about dating or marrying someone of a different race. Sure, you and your partner may encounter nasty quips from strangers, pushback from friends and family, and weird fetishy comments about your unborn children, but bragging about having a [insert race here] spouse is just not a good look. While my blackness is part of who I am, it's just that. A part. It doesn't define me as a person, and I sure as hell wouldn't be okay with Patrick describing me as his "black wife." I am his "loudmouth wife who laughs like a witch and is too fond of puns, but who I love anyway."

Strangers who won't mind their own business aren't the only people who have questioned my decision to shack up with a really nice lawyer who once took a seven-hour flight to Paris in dress shoes and a stuffy suit to surprise me with a wedding proposal. While many assume I was on the hunt for a "white kang," in reality I'd dated (aka slept with—sorry, Mom) all sorts of guys before Pat came along and became my first serious boyfriend.

Introducing him to my family was nerve-racking, and they didn't really make it easy. Right around the fateful anniversary video, I bought myself a new car after years driving a clunky old Volvo. My new Toyota Yaris was the first car I'd paid for entirely with my own money, and I was feeling very grown-up. My uncle, who'd lent me money a few times when I was in college and therefore got a kick out of teasing me about every adulthood milestone, called to congratulate me.

"Heard you got a new car. What color is it?" he asked.

"Blue!" I replied, beaming. I'd heard a weird statistic that red cars often had higher insurance rates, so I felt proud of myself for being responsible and picking something more sensible, even though I wasn't sure it mattered to Geico.

"I'm surprised it isn't white, to match your li'l boyfriend."

Yep, that's right—my uncle called me up and pretended to congratulate me on an achievement so that he could comment on the fact that my boyfriend was white. Not even really because he wanted to say anything about the fact that he was white—but it felt as if he wanted to make sure that I knew he was judging me. Even though he knew I wouldn't have been able to keep a white car clean to save my life.

Worse was my dad's account of meeting Pat for the first time. We'd been together for a few years, so our love was not some illicit wrong-side-of-the-tracks romance—we'd already moved to New York together and were in the "Why the fuck is the bathroom so disgusting?!" phase. I was visiting my father in South Carolina when I overheard him on the phone in his bedroom, saying something like "...and she brought this li'l *white boy* up in my house."

Don't ask me why the male members of my family liked to refer to Patrick, who is six feet tall and a smooth two-hundred-plus pounds, as "li'l," but to them that is what he was: insignificant, petty, silly. I stormed into my dad's bedroom and yelled at him to "GET OFF THE PHONE RIGHT NOW."

"How dare you say that about him?" I screamed like I was the lead actress in a drama about an interracial couple who were determined to fight for their love whatever the cost. "You don't know him! I love him! I respect him! And you should like and respect him because I do! He treats me right!"

My dad apologized immediately and said he was proud of me for "standing up for my man." I knew he meant it, but I also couldn't help but wonder if I'd always have to defend my relationship to my family.

ммммм

When black people are questioning the validity of my relationship, it helps, of course, that I don't have to make any excuses for Pat. There's always an assumption that, because he's white, Pat and I must have awkward problems discussing the uh, you know, *ahem*, political situation. Or assumptions that he mumbles racial slurs in his sleep as his subconscious fights to express how he really feels about the blacks. Sometimes people, thinking they've caught me, will ask, in a *gotcha!* tone, "Well...does he support Black Lives Matter?" To which I say: "Duh?" Even if you put aside the basic fact of my existence as a black person, social justice is a huge part of my career. I suppose there are couples who keep their personal and professional lives separate—if I were married to a physicist I doubt I'd be able to explain the intricacies of what he did every day—but "the police shouldn't kill black people" is not exactly quantum mechanics.

It's a little absurd that I have to recite my husband's social justice credentials to prove he's worthy of me—I'm a grown-ass woman who can make choices for herself. But more than a few people are willing to write me off as an activist because I'm married to a white guy, so here goes: Patrick is really empathetic, to the point that I can't even really complain to him about a woman cutting me off in line at the grocery store because his response is usually something like "Maybe she was just having a bad day. I'm sure she didn't mean it." I wouldn't marry anyone who didn't care about people, but his compassion is next level. (I'd like to say "I'd never even date anyone who didn't care about people," but my twenties were a dark time.) Early in our relationship, whenever I talked about the racism I dealt with in high school and college, he would always ask how he could support me. In law school, he interned at a public defender's office, and he's worked pro bono for survivors of domestic violence and people dealing with discrimination. When Mike Brown was killed in Ferguson, I would talk to Patrick about what was going on in the news, and he started using Twitter in earnest for the first time in order to follow live streams and other updates that mainstream news organizations weren't reporting on.

Once, he confided that one of his college friends had said I "went too hard about racism." Immediately, I got mad and starting yelling. "Well? So? What did you say?"

"I told him that you're passionate about racism because it affects your life, and that there's no such thing as going 'too hard' about inequality." And that, reader, is one of the many reasons I married him.

Pat is no longer friends with that guy, but it did make me wonder if other white people Patrick knows—or his family—have questioned his choice to marry someone who's so vocal about social justice and fighting white supremacy. And while I should be used to it by now, I doubt I'll ever grow tired of watching racist trolls and "men's rights activists" shit themselves over my wedding photos. "Who is this white man? Doesn't he know she HAAAAATES white men?!?!" they scream. When I see this, I just laugh, and then imagine their heads exploding, leaving what little brain matter they had to begin with splattered across their dank basement walls. I've made up my mind to stop wasting time or energy on these sorts of comments, but inevitably one of my fans will leap to my defense with "How can she hate white people when she has a white husband? Bloop!" Which instantly turns my self-satisfied cackling into a full-blown *oh no*.

While I appreciate followers having my back, the [insert race] partner defense deserves a swift retirement. Arguing "But I have a white husband" would make me no better than the proud bigots who trot out their "black ex-girlfriend" (who, let's be honest, probably doesn't exist) when someone calls them out on their racism. Of course I don't hate white people, but my husband isn't proof of that. If the ability to do the horizontal mambo automatically meant you shared a mutual understanding and respect for your "dance partner," my college years would've been a lot less depressing. But at the end of the day, who you befriend, date, marry, or get naked with doesn't say shit about your morals or understanding of privilege, oppression, or social justice. That's like a serial killer proclaiming, "I have plenty of friends who are alive!"

I often have to deal with people questioning the validity of my activism and blackness because of my marriage, but strangely enough, Patrick doesn't encounter nearly the same level of vitriol. (Try guessing why...) Occasionally he'll get online messages from anti–"social justice warriors" to the tune of "How can you be married to someone who hates the white race so much?" along with the occasional "cuck,"* but in general the harassment gets funneled through me. People don't feel the need to criticize a white man for his choices, but they assume, paradoxically, both (1) that they need to "warn" me about white men because I can't fend for myself, and (2) that I'm trying to single-handedly destroy the black race because I share a refrigerator with a white man.

Another moment in our relationship that illustrates this perfectly took place shortly after we got engaged. Two things happened: A bunch of Patrick's extended family added me on Facebook, and Obama was reelected. The night of his win, I posted something celebratory on Facebook—don't remember what. Suddenly, a photo I didn't really recognize popped up under my status update. A negative comment about Obama. I was deleting people left and right that night. I don't remember what was said; all I remember is hitting the trusty *Unfriend*. I realized she was Patrick's relative a minute later, when she messaged me: "You don't know what you're marrying into." Then she blocked me.

Adrenaline up from arguing with people all night, I asked Patrick what the FUCK that was supposed to mean. He admitted

---

*   Originating from the olde term "cuckold," which refers to a man whose wife is having sex with another man, "cuck" is an alt-right insult lobbed at a man who's perceived as weak. It's rooted in sexist stereotypes and toxic masculinity, of course.

he was as confused as I was and said he'd talk to her, and I completely forgot about it.

Fast-forward to about five years later, Pat's family reunion in Tennessee. I'm admittedly not a fan of the great outdoors, but I ended up having an amazing time; we went whitewater rafting and hiking during the day and played card games and drank moonshine late into the night. Although I knew only a handful of people at the start of the week, by the end of the trip we were all sharing funny stories and proudly wearing our family reunion T-shirts. It was nothing at all like the stereotypically dramatic family reunions portrayed on TV. It was great.

As we were getting ready to leave on the last day, when everyone was saying their goodbyes and making plans for the next meetup, one of Patrick's family members came up to me. "It was so great meeting you," she said. "I had such a good time and… I'm really happy for you." And then she started crying.

I was a little confused—had we connected in such a moving way? I couldn't remember us exchanging more than a few words, because she had been awfully quiet all week. I tried to go with it. Then she added, "I just want to apologize for everything. I feel so bad. The whole weekend I was thinking that you must hate me, and I'm just so sorry."

Now totally confused, I replied that it was great to meet her, too, and that there was nothing to apologize for. What was she talking about?

It didn't hit me until we got in the car to go to the airport that she was the girl from my Obama Facebook post, and that she had been so quiet because what she'd said to me had been weighing on her mind. Though I don't want to dismiss the very real and very awful racism that people sling online, I can't help thinking that this is how a lot of casual online racists would react IRL— ashamed and regretful. People are very bold on the internet; they are not bold in person.

Pat and I didn't start *Last Name Basis* because we wanted to make a podcast "about" being in an interracial relationship—sure, we talk about race and social issues, but we also gripe about our loud neighbors, tease each other relentlessly, argue over furniture, and share our funniest and most embarrassing New York adventures. In that way, it's a show about two people who love each other, even though they have different interests and don't always agree. If anything, the fact that he's white and I'm black should create more challenges—but it's only ever been an issue for other people, never for us.

I realize that we're more of an exception than the rule. Even couples who have everything in common have challenges and struggles; it's just not possible to always view everything through the same lens. Every week we field email questions from mixed-race couples struggling to communicate about race, privilege, politics, and not-so-secretly racist in-laws. Although our relationship is far from perfect, and although I don't believe in "marriage experts," I'm flattered that people look up to us and seek our advice.

Here's what I've learned: People will have opinions about your relationship no matter who you are or who you love. But it doesn't really matter if some guy in Oklahoma thinks your gay interracial relationship is a sign of the impending apocalypse, because you're not married to some guy in Oklahoma. As difficult as it may be, your energy is better served by focusing on the internal work: compromise, understanding, and growing together. That means giving your partner the grace to learn, just as you'd want them to do for you. Be honest about what you want and what your boundaries are. Don't put off the hard conversations; don't wait to talk about your morals, your politics, or your beliefs. Or your personal standards of bathroom cleanliness.

THE DEBATE

There's a lot of confusion on the internet about where my true allegiances lie. Am I racist against white people, or am I a traitor against black people? Am I "anti-white," or am I a "self-hating bed wench"?* Who do I hate more: Myself? White men? Black men? Or all men?

To settle the score once and for all, I decided to stage a debate, live, in front of an audience. Below is the complete transcript from the event.

FRANCHESCA RAMSEY: Good evening from the Reddit offices, located in the pits of hell. I'm Franchesca Ramsey, and I want to welcome you all to the first ever debate to determine my true essence. Am I a self-hater, a man-hater, or both? To help us answer this question, I've invited prominent leaders of two groups who've devoted countless hours to theorizing and speculating about the burning contents of my heart and loins. Please join me in welcoming noted men's rights activist (MRA) Colton Harris Gordon and a leading Twitter hotep, Dr. A. G. Stankofa.

[*Awkward applause. A hushed voice can be heard saying, "I thought this was going to be a screening of* Wonder Woman?"]

MRA, COLTON HARRIS GORDON: I welcome the opportunity to prove your commitment to white genocide.

RAMSEY: Whoa, whoa, whoa! Slow down there, Colton—we haven't started just yet!

---

*   *Bed wench* or *bed warmer* was a term used to describe black slave women who were forced to sleep in the master's bed for the purpose of "keeping it warm"—being used as a sex slave. Yeah, it's pretty gross.

HOTEP, DR. A. G. STANKOFA: Of course the white man finishes before we've even begun. Premature ejaculation is just one side effect of a savage diet. But you'd know all about that, wouldn't you, Chesca?

RAMSEY: I can't say I know anything about Colton's eating habits, but let's not get ahead of ourselves here. Tonight's debate will be divided into three segments. I will pose the same question to both of you, and you'll each have up to one minute to respond. We'll then close out the evening by taking questions from the audience before determining who has won the debate. And with that, let's get started!

First question: My husband! He's white. Dr. Stankofa, you're up first.

HOTEP: Unsurprising. Your melanin levels have clearly been depreciated because you share a bed with a white devil. These white demons age like milk, which is why they seek to drain the life-giving melanin from our queens. You hate yourself and your people so much that you abase yourself to be desecrated by the pasty curd sack you call a spouse.

RAMSEY: Thank you. I appreciate that feedback. Colton, same question.

MRA: I'd first like to say that the topic you've presented is not a question. Second, I'm in my mid-thirties, and people regularly assume I'm in my early thirties, so the milk-aging thing is patently false. Just one more example of black supremacist corporate media shills spreading lies about the white race—

RAMSEY [interjecting slyly]: I don't see age, so I wouldn't know.

MRA: I'll admit I was shocked when I learned Franny was married, let alone married to a white man. But upon further research it became clear that this "marriage" is an inside job. Nothing more than an advanced plot to eradicate the white race and subjugate white men under the guise of matrimony.

RAMSEY: So you're saying I'm smart, creative, and have excellent leadership skills? Duly noted.

Next question: Complete the following sentence: "Franchesca is a feminist because…"

Colton?

MRA: She hates men.

RAMSEY: Dr. Stankofa?

HOTEP: I'd have to agree with the alabaster bastard. But I'd add that Chesca hates men because she's never had the pleasurable fulfillment that can only be experienced when a female's brain is fertilized by a black man's royal obsidian.

RAMSEY: Interesting. What do you make of the argument that it's possible to advocate for racial equality and be in an interracial relationship?

Dr. Stankofa?

HOTEP: That sounds like some gay shit.

RAMSEY: And you, Colton?

MRA: I'm pretty sure I have a meme for that...give me a minute...

RAMSEY: Oops, your minute's up! Looks like that concludes tonight's debate—thanks to everyone for participating. I'm sure you'll all use the hashtag #WhiteGenobride on social media to let us know what you thought.

HOTEP: Hey, wait a minute. I thought we were ending with audience questions? This event is clearly rigged in the chalky gargoyle's favor.

RAMSEY: Oh, goodness! You're right! Let's go ahead and take one audience question to close out the evening.

AUDIENCE MEMBER: Hello. First, I'd like to say thanks for hosting such an enlightening and intellectually stimulating discussion, Franchesca. It's truly been delightful. So, I guess my question is, "Why can't either of you mind your own fucking business?"

[Audience applauds, then cues up their reaction GIFs.]

CHAPTER TWELVE
EULOGIES FOR CRINGEWORTHY COMMENTS

We are gathered here today to say goodbye to a list of comments that just won't accept that their time has come. If you've ever been brave enough to call out systems of oppression, whether in a one-on-one conversation or on a larger scale, you may have encountered some of these not-so-witty retorts. Born of racism, sexism, homophobia, transphobia, and/or simple ignorance, these reactions tend to be passive-aggressive, microaggressive, and gaslighting; they downplay arguments against bigotry so that the person committing it can save face or look smart. In reality, they make you look the opposite. They've been languishing for a while, so let's put them out of their misery once and for all.

1. COMMENT: "SORRY IF YOU'RE OFFENDED."

Often heard when: Someone has done something hurtful or offensive, and they don't understand (or care) why what they did was wrong. But they also don't want you to be mad at them.

Why it should be laid to rest: When "if" sneaks its way into an apology, it corrupts the entire thing from the inside out. Much like the "RE: URGENT DEAR SIR OR MADAM" email that somehow managed to slip past your spam folder, "sorry if" is highly suspicious. Humans are proud, often obnoxious creatures by nature—we hate apologizing, because apologizing means admitting we did something wrong. So we try to have our cake and eat it, too, by apologizing "if" we've offended anybody. That "if" is tricky—it suggests the person in question might not be offended, when in actuality the person has already clearly conveyed that they are. "Sorry if" also fails to take responsibility for the offensive words or behavior by making the apology conditional. To make matters worse, what comes after the "if" is just as pathetic: "Sorry if *you're offended*" is a cop-out because that comment "apologizes" for another person's feelings rather than owning up to what you did to cause those feelings. This is a non-apology masquerading as a real apology, and it's really condescending to boot.

Comeback: "There's no need for 'if'—I am offended. So are you sorry?"

2. COMMENT: "WHY ARE YOU SO ANGRY?"

Often heard when: You're angry. Which means you're dropping F-bombs and/or harshly worded opinions about injustice, oppression, or prejudice. Or you're just passionate about something and expressing that.

Why it should be laid to rest: "Why are you so angry?" and its bratty cousins "You're making a scene," "You're being hysterical," and "You need to calm down" are part of a broader phenomenon known as *tone policing*. Enacted by what's known as the Tone Police, tone policing is the offering of unsolicited advice on how to express one's feelings. The Tone Police claim expertise on topics they heard about on *The Wire* or in informational brochures for NGOs they contemplated volunteering for, and they do this by questioning the intensity of others' reactions to these topics. In turn, the Tone Police derail the conversation, away from the systemic wrong you were discussing and toward the validity of your response to that wrong. Another way to put what they're saying is "I feel uncomfortable when you feel comfortable feeling freely."

Why are they so uncomfortable with your feelings? Maybe it's because they feel complicit or guilty. Maybe it's because they really just don't get what it's like to connect with oppression in a personal way. They may need to be exposed to that anger to inspire and provoke action. Anger can bring awareness to the severity of an issue and be a meaningful part of one's education. Anger is a valid emotion, and it doesn't lessen or invalidate truth. Not to mention, emotional distance is not an option for many marginalized people, and telling them to calm down only increases the alienation they may feel in these moments.

Comeback: "I think people should be treated fairly. And when they're not, it makes me angry. Why aren't you angry at all?"

3. Comment: "Maybe if you stopped talking about this all the time, it wouldn't be such a problem."

Often heard when: A problem is being discussed.

Why it should be laid to rest: Awareness, education, and discussion are essential to understanding a problem before working toward a solution. But...that isn't always the case. Here are some issues we have definitely made successfully go away after ignoring them:

- Student loan debt

- Algebra homework

- The growing stack of dishes in the sink

- The New York City subway system

- That pesky burning sensation when you urinate

- The fact that your favorite jeans don't fit anymore

- Overdraft charges

    Comeback: "Maybe if I ignore my taxes they'll go away? It worked for Wesley Snipes and Lauryn Hill!"

4. COMMENT: "RACIST? I'M NOT RACIST! YOU'RE THE REAL RACIST!"

    Often heard when: You call out racism.

    Why it should be laid to rest: "I'm rubber and you're glue, whatever you say bounces off me and sticks to you" hasn't been a valid line of defense since elementary school.

    Comeback: "Just like talking about global warming doesn't make me a greenhouse gas, talking about racism doesn't make me a racist."

5. COMMENT: "STOP PLAYING THE VICTIM."

    Often heard when: You're expressing feelings of sadness, disappointment, or fear in response to injustice.

    Why it should be laid to rest: Unless you're performing in a community theater production of *Law & Order: SVU*, I'm not sure why anyone would willingly choose to play the victim. The word "play" implies a fun or enjoyable experience, but there's nothing fun about the very real pain associated with being mistreated. Only people who lack empathy would see victimhood as some kind of game or performance with ulterior motives.

    There's also little to gain from "pretending" to be a victim. For example, survivors of sexual assault who come forward often face harassment and abuse from strangers and those close to them alike; they get blacklisted and lose their jobs, and their motives are often questioned to the point that they recant their story to avoid the continued abuse. "Stop playing the victim" is yet again an example of someone feeling uncomfortable or threatened by the feelings associated with your lived experience. Just as you're allowed to feel angry about oppression or injustice, it's natural to express feelings of sadness or fear, especially if you're exhausted by the prospect of trying to keep up a brave face.

Comeback: "Victimhood is not a game. I don't get a prize for talking about my experience."

6. COMMENT: "DON'T YOU HAVE MORE IMPORTANT THINGS TO THINK ABOUT?"

Often heard when: You're talking about something that's important to you.

Why it should be laid to rest: Humans have large brains. That is why it's possible to care about all different types of things simultaneously, and why everyone's priorities are different. You might think petitioning the Olympic committee to make camel wrestling an Olympic sport is really important. Meanwhile, I didn't even know camel wrestling was a real thing. (It is.) But whatever you do with camels on the weekend doesn't stop you from also volunteering at your local animal hospital or donating money to cancer research. Plus, if you cared about every single pressing, dire, and horrible issue on earth all the time, at the same time, you would have a breakdown. You don't go to a concert and yell, "Hey! I know everyone's having fun at a concert, but climate change is happening!" Besides, by going to the concert, you're sort of participating in the unimportant thing you're saying people shouldn't be participating in, because you're at the concert. No?

Comeback: "Don't you have more important things to think about than what I should be thinking about?"

HOW to CARE ABOUT MORE THAN ONE THING at a TIME

MONDAY

50% - Ugh, Monday
15% - Coffee
10% - Work
10% - Gym
5% - Sexist coworker
5% - Instagram
5% - Office coat drive

TUESDAY

50% - Cute puppy
on the subway
15% - Something viral
on Facebook
10% - Work
10% - Coffee
10% - Trip to the gyno
5% - Douchebag
sexist coworker

WEDNESDAY

30% - Planning BFF
birthday drinks
25% - Emails to HR
10% - Resist urge to
punch sexist coworker
10% - Update résumé
10% - Senator calls
(Planned Parenthood, net
neutrality, gun control)
5% - Work
5% - Bathroom-mirror
selfies
5% - Gym

THURSDAY

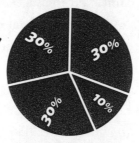

30% - Fuck this job
30% - It's my bestie's
birthday and I just quit
my job = DRINK
30% - How the hell do I
update LinkedIn?
10% - Does anyone
actually use LinkedIn?

FRIDAY

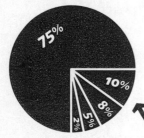

75% - Hungover
10% - Gatorade
8% - Where's my
other shoe?
5% - Instagram stories
2% - Shoe found!

7. COMMENT: "IT'S JUST A JOKE."

Often heard when: Someone is trying and failing to be funny, but succeeding at sounding like a bigot.

Why it should be laid to rest: People feel like using the word "joke" removes responsibility for the hurt their words may cause. It doesn't; in fact, it may make things worse. In an early episode of *Decoded*, "How Do You Handle a Racist Joke?" I talked about the difference between offensive jokes, which make people uncomfortable or mad or hurt their feelings, and oppressive jokes, which reinforce negative stereotypes about marginalized people, thus upholding the mistreatment of an entire group of people, not just an individual.

A Western Carolina University study found that when prejudiced attitudes around a marginalized group are shifting, negative jokes about that group can suggest discrimination is justified to people who may be on the fence. "Ironic" stereotyping—where the joker says something designed, allegedly, to mock sexists or racists or transphobes or homophobes—counts, too, so if anyone ever serves you with, "Political correctness is ruining comedy," the same stuff applies. It's just not funny to disrespect other people's beliefs, backgrounds, cultures, or identities when those are deeply rooted in longstanding oppression.

Many behaviors and practices that were once considered harmless jokes have since been recognized as irredeemably bigoted. For example: Blackface. In the past, a white actor covering their face in shoe polish and trotting out the worst stereotypes about black people was seen as comedic genius. That's because, at the time, black people didn't just lack positive representations of themselves in media; we weren't even considered human.

Jokes that punch down on marginalized people require no creativity because they've existed since the beginning of time. It's like telling a knock-knock joke and believing you're Richard

Pryor. That's why these "jokes" sound really old-fashioned and stale: They uphold the status quo by perpetuating harmful ideas about people who're already in vulnerable positions in society. Imagine what would happen if an elementary school principal went in front of the school and made fun of a seven-year-old. No matter how the student responded, the principal would automatically have the upper hand because they're older and in a position of power. Not only is this scenario completely unfair, it's also the plot of *Matilda*.

Comeback: [crickets] "Then why wasn't it funny? Maybe you can explain the joke to me."

8. COMMENT: "WELL, I DON'T SEE COLOR."

Often heard when: You're describing your experience as a person of color.

Why it should be laid to rest: People who say this usually mean well—they're attempting to let you know they're sooo not racist that they can't even conceive of a reality in which racism exists! But what they're actually saying is that racial *identity* is bad—not that racial oppression is bad. If someone is talking about their experiences as a person of color, "I don't see color" suggests their experiences aren't valid—or flat-out aren't real. If you wear glasses and I say, "I don't even see your glasses," that doesn't mean you suddenly have twenty-twenty vision—it just means I'm in denial. Or maybe that I need glasses myself.

A person's racial identity doesn't define them, but it does play a part in who they are. For many, "I don't see color" is an attempt to say "I don't see you as any different from me or anyone else," which is good in theory, but not realistic. People are different! And that's okay! Our differences aren't the issue. It's treating people as less than because of their differences that's the problem.

Comeback: "Well, even in black and white, I'm still a person of color."

9. COMMENT: "WHY DON'T THEY JUST COME HERE LEGALLY?"

Often heard when: You're talking about undocumented immigrants or the Deferred Action for Childhood Arrivals (DACA) program.

Why it should be laid to rest: If this question is being asked in earnest, the person you're talking to clearly has no idea how the American immigration system works. It is expensive, confusing, and prohibitive even for people who speak English as their native language, and who aren't dealing with the trauma of repressive governments and persecution. Besides, do you remember how this country was founded? Did Christopher Columbus come here legally? Did the Pilgrims have to make sure they had their passports open to the photo page so the line would move quickly at Plymouth Rock? Yes, there are immigration laws in place, but laws are not perfect. Part of our work, as activists and as citizens, is to determine what laws need to be refined and what new laws need to be created, and then to pressure our elected officials to act on that.

Comeback: "Why don't we just fix our broken immigration system so the people who want to come here legally can do so?"

10. COMMENT: "THE IRISH WERE SLAVES, TOO!"

Often heard when: You're discussing the repercussions of the transatlantic slave trade in today's modern world.

Why it should be laid to rest: When nearly two million Irish people immigrated to America during the Great Famine of the nineteenth century, they were abused, harassed, oppressed, and portrayed as diseased, poor rapists looking to steal American jobs. They were not, however, forced into slavery. The radical historian Noel Ignatiev's book *How the Irish Became White* describes how the population—many of whom came to America as indentured servants, under a system which, unlike slavery, was a voluntary arrangement, even if it was exploitative—were able to shed their nonwhite status and achieve equality by abusing black people and accepting racism. Let's agree that all persecution is bad, but not all persecution is equal.

Comeback: "No, they weren't!"

11. COMMENT: "THAT'S TERRIBLE. BUT MAYBE SHE SHOULD'VE . . ."

Often heard when: You're discussing sexual harassment or sexual assault.

Why it should be laid to rest: I'll never forget one particularly beautiful fall afternoon when a few of my female coworkers and I were sharing our best/worst street harassment stories. Normally, these storytelling sessions would happen in one of our offices, where we could comfortably splay across a couch surrounded by a mountain of decorative pillows featuring ironic sayings and nostalgic cartoons. (I never watched *Jem and the Holograms*, but I've always liked the artwork.) Anyway, on that crisp Wednesday, instead of gabbing in a private space, my lady friends and I were partaking in the ancient pastime of water-cooler talk in the kitchen for all to hear.

"Did you hear about the woman in Chicago?" one friend began. "Some guy asked for her phone number, and when she ignored him he stabbed her right there on the train. And then, instead of calling the police, everyone took out their phones and filmed it. It's terrifying. That's why I never take my headphones off."

Right on cue, a guy we'll call High-Key Jerk swooped in to

disabuse us of the naive notion that a woman who was stabbed—with a knife—for not giving a random guy her number had been wronged in some way.

"Don't get me wrong, that's fucked up. But I don't understand why more females don't just give dudes their number when they ask."

Oh man, that woman who got stabbed—why did she have to be such a buzzkill? She didn't have to answer his calls! And if he tracked her down to get revenge on her for not answering his calls, well, maybe she should've answered his calls.

While some of the details of that day are so clear—the sesame-and-onion scooped bagel halves we grazed on while sipping burned lattes from the office Keurig—the exact dialogue of our conversation escapes me. So I'm forced to paraphrase to the best of my ability here. I believe I said something along the lines of:

> What in the ever-loving fuck?

> Instead of asking why women can't be bothered to hand out their number to every dude with a fresh Cricket Wireless plan, why can't sensitive-ass man-babies learn how to take rejection without resorting to full-blown temper tantrums that end in physically harming women minding their gatdamb business?

High-Key Jerk was taken aback. But he recovered, and quickly hit me with a "Well, damn. See? This is what I mean. Clearly I caught you on your period." In that moment, he was like victim blaming: dead to me.

Unless you have a time-travel device handy, there isn't much value in theorizing how someone could've avoided being the victim of an assault of any kind. Maybe if I had worn a blue shirt instead of a red shirt, a bird wouldn't have pooped on me. See how ridiculous that sounds? Of course, it's extremely easy to suggest how a terrible situation or experience could've been avoided when (a) you haven't been in the situation; (b) you already know the outcome of the situation; (c) assigning blame makes you feel morally superior; or (d) all of the above. If someone is the victim of a crime, the CRIMINAL is responsible for committing the crime. They CHOSE to commit a crime.

Comeback: "You're right. It is terrible. If that criminal hadn't assaulted her she wouldn't have been assaulted."

12. COMMENT: "ALL LIVES MATTER."

Often heard when: Ugh (alternatively: any time someone even thinks about mentioning Black Lives Matter).

Why it should be laid to rest: I've saved the best (by which I mean worst) for last. "All lives matter" is the racist version of "I know you are but what am I"—an attempt to halt the conversation and engage in an endless back-and-forth. The Black Lives Matter movement was created in 2013 by Alicia Garza, Patrisse Cullors, and Opal Tometi in response to the acquittal of Trayvon Martin's killer, George Zimmerman. The movement is about creating a world where all lives—including black lives—matter equally. That's not the world we live in now, especially when we look at police violence and how it disproportionately affects black people. "All lives matter" is an empty retort designed to shut down conversations about black people and the issues they face. I think the "all lives matter" folks know that—they just refuse to admit it.

Comeback: "It's okay for a movement to be focused on a specific group or cause. 'Save the rainforest' doesn't mean 'Fuck all the other trees.'"

~~~~~~~~

Though we must say goodbye to these comments today, we realize that this will not be the last time we will be gathered here. As you go out into the world, you're bound to encounter any number of dismissive, ignorant, and hurtful statements that need to be peacefully laid to rest. With the understanding that a perfect eulogy is often hard to muster in the heat of the moment, we encourage you to set time aside to write a eulogy of your own so you'll be ready when you invariably usher other offensive quips onto the next plane in this circle we call life.

CHAPTER THIRTEEN

SELF-CARE IS NOT SELLING OUT (UNLESS IT IS)

The fact of their deaths, all at the hands of police officers, is heartbreaking. But it was the images and videos, which in the age of social media and the twenty-four-hour news cycle are all but unavoidable, that got to me. Trayvon Martin's body as the lede photo on a *Gawker* article called, "This, courtesy of MSNBC, is Trayvon Martin's dead body. Get angry." Philando Castile's blood splattered all over his car. Eric Garner being choked, tackled, and abused by police officers. Alton Sterling, in that red shirt, on the ground. All the beautiful shots of Sandra Bland smiling.

I've tried one too many times to avoid watching videos of black bodies being tormented and killed, but when you have to be on Facebook for work, it's almost impossible. When another police shooting happens, everyone immediately begins to share the story and comment on how awful it is, and with Facebook desperate to inflate its streaming numbers, of course the videos are set to autoplay. I remember the moment I felt like it had gone too far: There had been a string of police killings, one after another, and because I was working for *The Nightly Show* at the time I was required to watch the inevitable footage that followed so I could write about the news at work. But I began to find it hard to go on Facebook without breaking down. Since police brutality was being discussed more than ever, people began to post old videos of police shootings, too. I decided I didn't need to see any more black men bleeding out on my Facebook wall, so I went searching for instructions on how to disable autoplay.

They were surprisingly—or not, since Facebook is a company that makes money off you getting sucked in—hard to find. It was so hard that when I finally figured it out and could shield myself from watching Philando Castile bleed out next to ads for dog food and shoes, I typed up a quick post about how to disable autoplay on videos, thinking other people might need a break from the trauma like I did. It wasn't anything elaborate, just something along the lines of "There's a lot of shit going on right now, and you're probably seeing really graphic videos on Facebook. If you don't want them to play automatically, here's how to turn it off."

Someone more famous than I am once told me that when you hit 200,000 fans on Facebook, it's like the company flips a switch and assigns the most ridiculous, hateful people to comment on every one of your posts. When I wrote what I thought would be a harmlessly helpful post, I had around 250,000 followers, and criticism was swift and relentless. How dare I "sell out" like this? I was "ignoring the realities of police brutality." And worse— I was encouraging my fans to do the same. I was, once again, "canceled."

It's always strange to me when people start dictating what you must or must not do to be a good black person, a good feminist, a good advocate. Do I have to keep a tally of my activist points to prove I've earned a moment of rest? It feels gross to do so. I had just written a piece about Castile for *The Nightly Show* that went viral. I did live broadcasts for Facebook discussing police brutality. About a year and a half before, I'd gone on Katie Couric's Yahoo show and screamed at former NYPD commissioner Ray

Kelly when he claimed the number of people who were killed by police officers was "infinitesimal." After the broadcast I was added to the show's "do not call" list, which is a nice way of saying I was banned from ever going on that show again. And yet commenters were saying I was betraying my people because I didn't want to watch graphic videos of them being senselessly murdered every hour of the day. I understand that some white people need to see the horrible visual evidence of police brutality to realize the gravity of the situation, and even that they need to see it over and over. But not everyone needs repeated, in-your-face confirmation to understand that something abhorrent is happening and that they need to do something about it.

I consider what I was doing with that Facebook post an act of self-care, a practice that has been criticized a lot lately, and rightly so. (I'll get to that.) "Self-care" originated as a medical term that, before the civil rights and women's movements of the 1960s and '70s, was used in the context of mentally ill and elderly patients, who were advised to practice healthy living habits in addition to their outside treatment. Then it was applied to people who work high-stress, emotionally taxing jobs, like EMTs and social workers. It was only natural that this concept would appeal to activists who were fighting for social justice, especially since so much of that work dealt with the ways society restricted, commodified, and controlled marginalized bodies. In her 1988 essay collection, *A Burst of Light*, Audre Lorde wrote, "Caring for myself is not self-indulgence, it is self-preservation, and that is an act of political warfare."

Today, the line has been quoted again and again by activists wrestling with a political situation that, in some ways, doesn't seem so different from the way it was thirty years ago. When it seems that so much of society would rather you not live at all, keeping yourself healthy is a revolutionary act. In the case of police violence in particular, research has shown that black people experience PTSD symptoms when they see brutal images of black death. (Monica Williams, the clinical psychologist and director of the Center for Mental Health Disparities at the University of Louisville, calls this "vicarious trauma.") Stories of racism passed down over generations mean trauma is passed down, too.

Combined, these things take a toll, especially as it's so easy to see how black death has become fodder for gruesome entertainment. We don't parade victims of tragedies around when they aren't black. After the mass shooting at a concert in Las Vegas in October 2017, videos were shared, but they quickly faded away, and they were never so horrifying as what has become typical after any police shooting. When the TV anchor Alison Parker was fatally shot at point-blank range on camera, it aired live, and after that news stations decided they weren't going to show the footage anymore. I agree with both of these decisions—people were stressed and sad and angry after these incidents, and watching them replay over and over only exacerbates these feelings. But why can't we show the same care and consideration for black victims? (I think you know the answer.)

Taking care of yourself doesn't mean that you're not also doing important work that advances the causes that are important to you; in fact, it's a critical part of doing that work. Without self-care, you burn out—physically, but also through something known as "compassion fatigue," which is basically just what it sounds like: When you focus too much time and energy on others in distress, you start to wear down, too. Which eventually means you have to stop doing work altogether.

I get why people are skeptical of self-care. For a while there, it seemed like it had been stripped entirely of its meaning and existed only as a marketing tactic. As I've watched the YouTube beauty community change, I can see how "self-care" has become shorthand for "buy these products." It's not uncommon to hear an influencer declare, apparently without shame, "A big part of my self-care practice is doing a hydrating skin mask once a week. Which is why I wanted to start my own line of hydrating skin masks, starting at thirty dollars for two ounces." This is partially why it's become something to criticize people for: It's assumed that if you're posting about going to a movie, or getting your nails done, or buying a candle, you aren't doing anything else (except maybe shilling for some candle company).

But you don't have to throw the baby out with the bathwater. (Or the pedicures out with the...dirty foot-bath water?) The rise of self-care as a marketing tool makes it difficult to discern between legitimate rest and performative activism, but that doesn't mean you have to stay plugged into the news and angry 24/7. Haters will claim you're doing yourself and the movement a disservice by not staying ON all the time, but in fact you'd be doing yourself and the movement a disservice if you were.

So now I'm sure you're on the edge of your seat, wondering: *What does Franchesca do when she needs to chill out? I must know!*

Here are a few of my favorite things to do when I need to relax:

- **Hour-long foot massages.** I recently discovered that I love foot massages, which are not something I expected I would like, so I've been doing that. (Despite what my husband says, my feet aren't gross, but I still tip a lot.) If you factor in the minutes it takes you to get used to having your feet handled by a stranger and then the minutes it takes to clear your head of other stresses, you realize that's still a solid forty-three-minute rubdown.

- **Journaling.** It's nice to have a moment to reflect on and process your day, and lately I've gotten into drawing in my journal—trying to make the page pretty is soothing, both because pretty things are soothing and because it forces me to concentrate on one thing rather than letting my thoughts race. Fun markers and stickers aren't necessary, but I buy them anyway. I challenge myself to make every page different. Sometimes I take the traditional approach and reflect on what happened that day; other days I make a collage of words and quotes that inspire me, or make lists of things I'm thankful for or things that made me laugh that day. It's a nice way to unwind, and it's also nice to have a record of what you do every day. One warning: I would say that going back and reading your journals from high school is actually the opposite of self-care. I went through a few of my high school notebooks thinking it would be good to quote them in this book, but no. All I did was say I was fat and keep daily charts of how much weed I smoked.

- Speaking of weed: I **quit smoking** it. This one might seem a little confusing, since I'm citing no longer doing something as a form of self-care, but I promise it makes sense. I started smoking weed with friends in high school and later graduated to smoking alone out my bedroom window, eventually becoming the self-crowned queen of wake-and-bake. Even though I spent 85 percent of my senior year of high school stoned, I managed to keep a high grade point average, so I didn't see any harm. When my mother would ask about the strange smell, I assured her it was a candle. (Sorry, Mom, Fresh Grass is not one of Bath and Body Works' signature scents.)

  Through college and after graduation, weed continued to be my go-to way to unwind or fill the time when I was bored. In my mid-twenties, when I moved to New York and was struggling to figure out what I was doing with my life, it became a crutch. I'd feel sad about my career, so I'd smoke weed and waste my day online instead of writing, auditioning, or doing much of anything. Once my career started to take off, I'd smoke to temper my anxiety.

But as I got older, it stopped working, and eventually it started to make my moods worse. I went from being a chill, funny, and happy stoner who was always pretty productive while high to being oversensitive, paranoid, and extremely emotional, sometimes unable to do anything but sleep. I'd always loved cracking jokes and talking shit with Patrick, but suddenly when I was stoned, any little comment would set me off and I'd dissolve into tears. Patrick started to notice a pattern. "Wait. Did you smoke?" became his catchphrase the minute we'd start to argue or I'd take a joke too seriously. I realized that pot was transforming me into someone I didn't recognize and that I needed to cut back. Finally, as I was battling a cold during my 2015 Christmas vacation, I took a few hits at a party and almost instantly lost my voice. I couldn't talk for almost two weeks. I took it as a sign and decided to quit then and there.

It still feels weird to come home from a long day and not unwind with a joint. Sometimes I do miss it. Or maybe I just miss how getting high used to make me feel. Either way, recognizing that smoking pot doesn't make me feel good anymore was the first step toward letting it go as a way to take care of myself.

- **Coloring.** The adult-coloring boom of 2014 came and went for many, but I've stuck with it and I'm so glad I have. I've generated a pretty big collection ranging from intricate celestial designs to impressively complicated abstract mazes. (One of my favorites is *I Love My Hair*, which is illustrated by my dear friend Andrea Pippins.) One year, I brought my coloring books on a trip to Costa Rica with Patrick and a few of our couple friends. My plan was to spend every afternoon on the beach coloring while sipping a bright, fruity drink—this is my vision of bliss. On the first day, I spread my books out on the dining room table, and all the husbands, including Patrick, snickered. What grown woman has ten different coloring books and more than a hundred colored pencils? And brings them on her beach vacation? This grown woman, 'cause she can do whatever she wants. By the end of the trip, I had to pry the animal-kingdom coloring book from Patrick's hands and promise to get him a copy of his own when we got back to the States.

- **Working out.** Nothing is better at distracting you from your problems than sweat stinging your eyes as you try to get your ass up for two more burpees.

- **Face masks.** Though face-mask selfies have become a warning sign of someone who may be selling face masks on Instagram, that doesn't mean they're worthless. Even if they don't have an effect on your skin—and for some I'm seriously skeptical—they force you to sit still and not do anything for ten to fifteen minutes. I especially enjoy those that you have to let dry before you peel them off. It's extremely satisfying to see how big of a piece you can pull off without ripping it.

Everyone's version of self-care is different. But no matter your chill-out method of choice, it's important to make self-care a regular practice when things are going good, so that when things aren't so hot you can prioritize keeping yourself (relatively) calm because the practice will be a habit. It's similar to when you're like, "Okay, I have to get up for work at eight a.m., which sucks because I like to stay up until two thirty reading Oh No They Didn't! (my longtime guilty-pleasure gossip community) on LiveJournal. I'm going to try to get up at eight a.m. on the weekends, too, so it'll be easier to pull myself away from the Taylor Swift walking posts [don't judge me] during the week."

CONCLUSION

ACTIVISM IS LIKE LONG DIVISION — YOU HAVE TO SHOW YOUR WORK

As excited as I was for the opportunity to write a book, I was also really nervous. The prospect of reliving some of the embarrassing, ignorant, or even offensive things I've said and done was daunting, especially since I've made a career of, literally, decoding injustice. Some people—fans and haters alike—have a perception of me as some kind of all-knowing, holier-than-thou social justice oracle, making pronouncements on bigotry from my production studio atop a mountain. It's not an accurate perception, but the idea of disappointing people scared me shitless. And not in an "Oh God, I really needed to shit and now I feel a lot better" way—more like "Oh God, I think some of my intestines might have just slipped out."

Writing was especially anxiety inducing because every time I sat down to work, I would get stuck thinking about how every word could be twisted or misinterpreted. These worries weren't unfounded, either; it's not like when you ask your friend, "Hey, does this outfit make me look like a *Real World* cast member circa 2004?" even though you know it doesn't. The world is an unwieldy place these days, and my little corner of it—the internet—is particularly stressful. It allows people to make anonymous claims without any repercussions; many social media users seem dedicated to taking your words out of context to make you look stupid, or worse. Add the fact that we're often talking about life-and-death issues for people who haven't had the chance to advocate for themselves, and you have a ticking time bomb.

I'm not sure I could call myself an expert in anything other than styling my hair and bad puns, but I truly believe that trying to get it right is worth something. So now that you've laughed at, consumed, and side-eyed all my mistakes, accomplishments, and hard-won lessons, what's next?

UNDERSTAND AND ACKNOWLEDGE YOUR PRIVILEGE

Although I've used it myself, these days the phrase "check your privilege" makes me cringe. It's certainly worthwhile to reflect on how your privilege can get in the way of your understanding and empathy. But "check your privilege" is usually spit out as a contemptuous demand instead of a helpful suggestion, like when you go to a restaurant and they ask if you'd like to "check your coat," and then you remember, *Oh, right, I have a coat on, and I would like to leave it here so that I may enjoy my dinner without it hanging off the back of my chair and collecting dust off the floor.* If a member of the waitstaff barked at me to check my coat, or *else*, I would probably leave the restaurant, write a bad Yelp review, and tell all my friends never to eat there again, even if they served the best steak in the world.

Just as being ordered to check my coat would put me off eating at Rude Kitchen, aggressive commands that people check their privilege can backfire, too. What if the person you're talking to has no idea what "privilege" means? Left to figure it out for themselves, they probably assume you think they're rich, or that they've never struggled or had to work hard. The conversation will veer off course because they'll feel the need to tell you about their parents getting divorced when they were in third grade and about the summer that they broke their leg and had to sit by the pool with their foot propped up while their brothers and sisters learned to tread water. I've never broken a bone, but my parents got divorced when I was six, so I can empathize. But broken bones and broken marriages don't erase the privileges of, say, an able-bodied straight person who just said something really ignorant and hurtful about same-sex marriage, or who slid their able-bodied ass into the only wheelchair-accessible bathroom stall because they wanted to use the "better mirror."

In an effort to help others understand their privilege and how it shields them from certain experiences, I've found that talking about my own privilege can open up the conversation. How can I possibly support trans people if I'm unwilling to see how being cis impacts my daily life, from my access to things like health care services, safe housing, and public restrooms to the fear of being harassed or abused while walking down the street? How can I push for more accessible spaces if I don't understand how being able-bodied affects how I move through the world?

In my animated video "Sometimes You're a Caterpillar" (illustrated by the wonderful artist and activist Kat Blaque) I use a story about a caterpillar and a snail to explain privilege. The caterpillar and the snail are best friends who live in a garden together, and one day they decide to go to a party on the other side of the fence. But they quickly realize that there's a problem: While the caterpillar is able to crawl under the fence, the snail gets stuck because of her shell. It's not the caterpillar's fault that the snail gets stuck under the fence, but it would be rude as hell for him to say something like "Hurry up! I don't even see your shell." And while the caterpillar can easily fit under the fence, he still has his own challenges, like having to find shoes for all sixteen of his feet. The bugs both live in the same garden, but they move through it very differently. When the snail patiently explains that she just can't fit under the fence, the caterpillar has to check his privilege—and then they work together to figure out how to get to the party before the keg is tapped.

KEEP IT INTERSECTIONAL

A few years ago, I made a video in which I dressed up as a drag queen and walked through the streets of New York City asking people to guess whether I was a man or a woman. It was meant to be a comedic "social experiment" that loosely touched on sexism and gender stereotypes. What it actually was—though I didn't realize it at the time—was pushing a transphobic narrative, implying that it's totally okay to ask invasive questions about a stranger's genitals. The idea that trans people are oddities for us to gawk at is an extremely harmful one, and it's a huge part of the reason trans people, and especially trans women, are at such a high risk for violence: People demand to know "what's down there" and then fly off the handle if they don't get an answer, or if they don't get the answer they want. I'd made an all-too-common mistake: I was unable to see my privilege as a cis person and had thrown my trans brothers and sisters under the bus. I was trying to make a funny, socially conscious video about gender stereo-types, but I had forgotten that those same stereotypes I was toy-ing with affect trans people very differently.

Intersectionality is the study of how different systems of oppression overlap. People are multidimensional, and race, class, gender, sexuality, and ability play different roles in how we move through the world. The sexism I deal with as a straight cis black woman is often intertwined with racism; my experiences are going to be different from those of a cis white lesbian woman who deals with sexism that's often intertwined with being fetishized or discriminated against based on her sexuality. So it's crucial that our activism isn't just about the people who look like us.

Unfortunately, well-meaning, smart, socially conscious (or "woke") people often forget to make space for marginalized people whose experiences differ from their own. From gay men calling their female friends "sluts" or "bitches," to white women claiming that their experience of sexism is equivalent to another person's experience of racism, to reproductive rights movements forgetting that cis women aren't the only people who use birth control, to protest venues lacking wheelchair accessibility, and to social justice videos posted without captions, intersectionality fails are everywhere. Avoiding them requires care, consciousness, and a dose of humility, but it's worth it to build the world you want to live in. Because if your activism isn't intersectional, it's not really activism.

DO YOUR HOMEWORK

There will always be things you don't know and experiences you don't understand. It's okay to ask questions. Sometimes you'll be lucky enough to have someone who's willing to answer your questions or point you in the right direction of a book, movie, or article that you should check out for more information. But at some point you have to take responsibility for your own education. It's exhausting to always hold others' hands until they learn how to not be terrible people, especially when you're not getting paid for it. If you were in high school and wanted the smartest kid in English class to write a paper for you, you wouldn't expect her to do it for free. Not only is that cheating, it's exploitative.

If you do have a friend who's been kind enough to help you through your social justice education, the very least you can do is to get them a glazed doughnut to show your appreciation. (Better yet, take them out to dinner—though you should avoid Rude Kitchen.) But there are so many resources available if you actually want to learn, and at some point your racism tutor is going to be like, "Actually, I need to wash my hair tonight," and you'll have to take responsibility for your own education. Don't hesitate to hit up Google—and not just Wikipedia—or your local library or bookstore.* Do your own research on the issues and communities you're looking to support. I'm calling it homework for a reason.

KNOW WHEN TO CALL OUT, AND MAKE SPACE TO CALL IN

If you are neutral in situations of injustice, you have chosen the side of the oppressor.

—Desmond Tutu

You know those ads in the subway that say "If you see something, say something"? The same applies to activism. It's critical that you use your voice to call attention to harmful or oppressive forces, including but not limited to celebrities, TV shows, movies, Halloween costumes, and cartoons with secret racist messages. You can't just sit back and remark quietly to your similarly liberal friend, "My, that's just awful." When the offense is public, it usually deserves a public condemnation.

But just as often as we publicly speak out about what's important to us, we should also make an effort to pull individuals aside and lovingly guide them toward the right path when they mess up. We all have that one friend who's willing to keep it real with you when you get a bad haircut, who will discreetly make a tooth-picking motion at you when no one else has the guts to tell you about the piece of spinach stuck in your teeth. Sometimes you have to be that friend.

---

* Some of my favorite books to get you started: *A People's History of the United States* by Howard Zinn; *The New Jim Crow: Mass Incarceration in the Age of Colorblindness* by Michelle Alexander; *Ain't I a Woman: Black Women and Feminism* by bell hooks; *We Should All Be Feminists* by Chimamanda Ngozi Adichie; *Redefining Realness: My Path to Womanhood, Identity, Love and So Much More* by Janet Mock.

If you have a friend or family member who says something offensive, remember that there were times when you screwed up and someone in your life had the grace to pull you aside instead of embarrassing you in front of everyone. Remember that you, too, were once exposed to something that changed your thinking and made you a better person. Wouldn't it feel good to be that something for someone else?

SPEAK UP, NOT OVER

Use your privilege to advocate for marginalized folks, especially when you're in spaces where marginalized folks aren't present. I wish it weren't the case, but people are more willing to listen to someone who has something in common with them. You probably have access to people whom I will never have access to, just as I have access to people you'll never have access to. By that same token, it's important to use your privilege to bring people who don't look like you into those spaces. How do we get more POC involved in this organization? Why aren't there any LGBTQ folks on our advisory board? Who can we hire to interpret for the event? What can we do to cultivate female leadership? Take a look at who's at the table, and then use your voice to offer a seat to someone who deserves to be there.

When marginalized people *are* around, resist the urge to center your voice and speak over them. Think of Destiny's Child. There are three members, wearing matching outfits, but Beyoncé's outfit is always the cutest. Everyone's doing the same choreography, but Bey is out front. Everyone gets a chance to sing a line or two, but...we know who the lead vocal is. In this analogy, you are Michelle or Kelly (pick your favorite), and the person whose humanity is being questioned or undermined or attacked, the one most qualified to give voice to their experience, is Beyoncé.

The first time I used this analogy I got some pushback: I was accused of being unfair to Michelle and Kelly, two very talented, beautiful women who no doubt have more success and higher credit scores than I could ever hope to. But I think the comparison works. When Michelle decided to pursue a career in gospel music, Kelly and Beyoncé were featured on her single, "Say Yes," and appeared in the song's music video; this time, Michelle took the lead—she even got the cutest outfit—and the others were there to support her. And when Kelly published her book of advice for new moms, Beyoncé and Michelle were at her book launch—not hogging the spotlight, but cheering Kelly on.

OWN YOUR MISTAKES, AND COMMIT TO CHANGE

No one is perfect, and I promise, you're going to screw up. But screwing up is an opportunity for you to be honest about your mistakes, learn from them, and move forward.

One thing that I've learned during my time in the trenches of content creation is that genuine apologies are very, very rare. If you can perfect the art of saying sorry, more often than not people will be willing to give you a second chance. A genuine apology is made up of two parts: (1) taking responsibility for what you've done, and (2) committing to change. Pretty simple, but most people tend to fall back on some version of "I'm sorry if you were offended," or "Well, I'm sorry you feel that way," or "It wasn't my intention to offend you." Unless you're a dominatrix who insults and offends people for a living because that's what your clients pay you to do, you rarely intend to offend people. Just because you didn't mean to do something doesn't change the result of what you actually did. As I've said before, if I step on your foot and break your toe, I didn't mean to break your toe, but your toe is still broken, and I'm sure you'd like to go to the hospital instead of listening to me explain that I didn't mean to break your toe.

We did an episode of *Decoded* about the excuses people make for slavery in response to Bill O'Reilly flipping out when Michelle Obama said the White House was built by slaves. Michelle was right, of course, but the incident inspired a great conversation about why people are so hesitant to acknowledge how slavery has played a role in our nation's history. In the episode, we mentioned the Holocaust and Berlin's Memorial to the Murdered Jews of Europe as an example of a way a nation has paid tribute to and respected a horrific time in history. We then compared that to the way America tends to frame slavery as something that happened in the past and doesn't need to be discussed anymore.

At the time, it seemed like an appropriate comparison. But soon after the episode went live, a number of viewers contacted me to express their disappointment that we'd used the Holocaust as a rhetorical device. Of course, I didn't intend to offend anyone—I didn't realize that it was actually anti-Semitic to use the Holocaust in this way, especially because people do it so often. But I realized that using this very painful piece of history as a way to prop up or give more importance to another cause—while completely disregarding that there are living Holocaust survivors, and that there are still people affected by the Holocaust and rampant anti-Semitism—suggests that anti-Semitism is a thing of the past. It also continues to push the idea that America was not complicit in the Holocaust in any way. After being called out and called in, we made an episode about the myths around the Holocaust and anti-Semitism, and we used the way I screwed up in the slavery episode as an example. People ended up really enjoying the segment—not just because it was informative, but because I owned up to my mistake, took the steps to remedy it, and used the experience to help other people.

All that said, keep in mind that forgiveness takes time; offering an apology doesn't mean it's automatically going to be accepted or that the hurt will magically disappear. An apology has to be combined with action to make a real impact, so remember to give people space to see your follow-through.

BAKE YOUR OWN COOKIES

> Racism should never have happened and so you don't get a cookie for reducing it.
> —Chimamanda Ngozi Adichie, *Americanah*

I love this quote, and I think it can be applied to all forms of social advocacy. Too often, people want credit for doing the right thing instead of just wanting to do the right thing. I don't want to be picky about acts of goodness, because the world needs more of them, but doing the right thing isn't always going to come with a badge or a pat on the back or a tray of warm cookies. Those invisible acts of advocacy are just as important, if not more so, than the hashtag campaigns and the epic racist takedowns. No one is going to be there to watch you explain to your uncle why football players are kneeling during the national anthem, but those conversations still need to happen.

Sometimes people will email me screenshots of terrible things their friends or family members have said—not because they called them out or called them in, but because they want to demonstrate how superior they are for not holding those same bigoted or outdated beliefs. Instead of running to show someone else how progressive and forward-thinking you are, you should be doing the work. You have to bake your own cookies. On the bright side, you can put whatever you want in them—no more gross white chocolate macadamia for you.

ACTIVISM IS LIKE LONG DIVISION—YOU HAVE TO SHOW YOUR WORK

Ultimately, being an activist is going to require way more time and discomfort than it takes to change your Twitter profile pic to a rainbow or put a safety pin on your backpack. These can be great signs of solidarity and support—well, maybe not the safety pin—but they're the bare minimum. You have to take the next steps to get out of your comfort zone and commit to continuously working to be a better person and, in turn, making the world a better place. That means getting involved in local politics, supporting diverse businesses and companies, passing the mic to marginalized folks, and giving your time, knowledge, and resources to charitable causes and organizations.

Here's where I'd insert a really clever calculus analogy, but truth be told, I never took calculus. It looked really hard and boring, and buying one of those TI-84 calculators seemed like a waste of money (especially when I could already play *Snake* on my Nokia phone). Instead, I'll say that activism is like long division: It consists of multiple steps, it's easy to mess up, and when you inevitably do make a mistake, the only way to find it and fix it is to show your work.

What does that mean, exactly? It's different for everyone. Because the internet has become a place where so many people feel comfortable talking about their identities, struggles, and personal experiences, people are very cynical about what it means to be an internet activist. But being vocal about issues you care about doesn't mean that's the only form your activism takes. Sure, some people use the internet as an easy way to perform "wokeness." But at the same time, there are few better ways to get the word out about an issue than talking about it online.

It can be hard to tell the difference between performative

social consciousness (known as "slacktivism") and legitimate activism. Often the categories overlap, and they can both involve getting the word out and expressing pride or outrage or sadness on social media. There are also some people who use the internet because they're not able to be vocal IRL. Maybe they live in a conservative community, or with conservative parents who will kick them out of the house if they come out as gay. Maybe they have a disability and can't join a march or sit-in. Maybe they have more than one job and can't afford to boycott certain companies.

Ultimately, showing your work is about being accountable to yourself, and about being able to demonstrate how you got where you are. You can't just write down a bunch of numbers and symbols and expect to solve a math problem—just ask my high school algebra teacher—and you can't just *say* you're an activist. Telling people you support LGBTQ folks is good, but you have to be able to explain how and why you support LGBTQ folks, whether it's by initiating a difficult conversation when a family member uses a slur or by voting in your local election when there's an anti-trans bathroom law on the ballot. How did you arrive at your perspective? To use another sort of flimsy math metaphor, how do you solve for x? While it's as important as ever to hold each other accountable, we also have to remember that everyone's journey is different, and learning takes time. If we want to figure out how to solve this, we have to do it together.

FRANCHESCA'S SIMPLE EXPLANATIONS OF NOT-SO-SIMPLE CONCEPTS

Congratulations! You've made it through all the stories about my life and internet drama without throwing the book across the room. I hope. Or maybe you got to page 12, didn't understand what the hell I was talking about, and came here for answers. Either way, I thought it would be helpful to clarify some of the terms and phrases I use in *Well, That Escalated Quickly*. I've seen firsthand that people can sometimes get a little (or a lot) judgy when it comes to not knowing certain tenets of social justice theory. But you have to learn sometime, and there should be no shame in confusion or asking for help. Having access to this kind of knowledge is a privilege in itself—just as having the time to read a book is. Not everyone has been exposed to these ideas. You don't know what you don't know, and you don't know how much your experiences (or lack thereof) influence you. Think about all the totally wrong stuff you believed as a kid: When I went to Catholic school, I thought that being gay was a sin—just like premarital sex. I also only listened to R&B because, as logic dictates, alternative rock was the devil's music, and it seemed very obvious to me that Green Day was corrupting our youth. Meanwhile, I blithely sang along to a song that goes "Step back, you're dancing kinda close / I feel a little poke comin' through" whenever it came on the radio. Life is full of realizations.

This is not intended as a comprehensive list of every term you'll need to know if you want to wade into activism, but it should work as a jumping-off point, especially if you want to talk to friends or family about these topics IRL. I'd encourage you to look up these concepts in actual books, at the actual library. The internet is an imperfect tool, and is often wrong; if you do go online for more info, you should read more than one source—no "just skimming." These concepts are serious, and important to a lot of people. It's worth it to do your due diligence.

Ableism—discrimination against people with disabilities, including through language.

Ally—someone who actively works to support the rights of marginalized groups they're not a part of.

Alt-right—framed as an "alternative" branch of conservatism, the alt-right is an internet-savvy rebranding of white supremacy. With prominent young figureheads like Richard Spencer and a penchant for memes, the movement paints its members as edgy, "anti-establishment" crusaders against "political correctness" and saviors of the white race.

Black Lives Matter—a black-centered activist movement started by Alicia Garza, Patrisse Cullors, and Opal Tometi after George Zimmerman was acquitted for the murder of Trayvon Martin in July 2013. Originally a hashtag, the movement gained steam as it raised awareness and organized protests around ending systemic violence against black people.

People often misunderstand the purpose of Black Lives Matter by assuming it's an exclusionary movement; it's not. It's a movement that focuses on the needs of marginalized people, and it doesn't shy away from centering those needs. That's why it's called Black Lives Matter and not "All Lives Matter" (see page 202). It's not about taking value away from white lives; it's about making black lives as valuable as white lives. Think of it this way: The existence of gay bars doesn't mean there are no straight bars. It's just that most bars are straight bars, and gay folks deserve spaces where they can safely and freely do their thing, too.

Black supremacy—not a thing.

Body positivity—the movement to normalize and accept bodies of all different shapes, sizes, and abilities in a world that privileges people who are thin, gender-conforming, able-bodied, and conventionally attractive.

Call in—to initiate a one-on-one conversation, out of public view, in order to make another person aware of their bigoted speech, behavior, etc. (see page 61).

Call out—to publicly bring attention to another person's bigoted speech, behavior, etc. (see page 56).

Censorship—a lot of people don't seem to get this one, so pay attention. The First Amendment says it is unconstitutional for the government to suppress speech it deems offensive, unacceptable, or a moral danger. Private individuals or groups can censor speech, usually through pressure like boycotts; that is not illegal. It is not an infringement of your rights when:

- I block you on Twitter.

- A newspaper drops your opinion column.

- You lose a book deal or yogurt sponsorship because you said something sexist or racist.

Centrist—a person or viewpoint that attempts to "see both sides" of a given issue or scenario, even when there is no comparison between both sides because one side is absolutely unacceptable. Often comes from a place of moral superiority or belief in pragmatism that is rarely borne out in reality. Example: After the Charlottesville Unite the Right rally, which was held in protest of the city's plan to remove a statue of Robert E. Lee, Donald Trump rejected violence on "all sides," though only the far-right protesters were at fault.

Cisgender (Cis)—denotes a person who identifies with the gender they were assigned at birth. For example: You are cisgender if, when you were born, the doctor said, "It's a girl!" and you still agree with that assessment.

Classism—the overt or subtle discrimination against lower-class people, often promoted through the willful ignorance of the realities of capitalism and poverty. Examples of classism include statements like "If you wanted health insurance, maybe you shouldn't have bought that iPhone" and the practice of restricting which foods people who receive government assistance can buy.

Colorblindness—the imaginary condition of not being able to "see race." While some people are literally unable to differentiate among certain colors, the comment "I don't see color" is often used figuratively to shut down or dismiss conversations about race and racism by suggesting the speaker sees everyone equally. But there's nothing wrong with seeing someone's race; it's part of who they are, and it shapes their experiences and worldview. The problem is treating someone *differently* because of their race.

Consent—permission that you give another person to engage in behaviors that require your involvement. Though it's usually used in sexual situations, you may also be asked to give your consent to police to search your property if they do not have a warrant.

Cultural appropriation—lots of people have tried to define cultural appropriation, and they haven't done a very good job.

It's the practice of majority groups taking cultural practices, imagery, clothing, or other things from marginalized people without attribution, often for profit, and without being respectful of the customs' cultural origins. Meanwhile, people from those marginalized groups are often stigmatized for or downright prohibited from engaging in their practices by society at large.

Appreciation, which involves respect, is not the same as appropriation, which doesn't. Going to a Mexican restaurant and participating in that culture is good; wearing a sombrero and saying you're going as "Mexican" for Halloween is not. Another way to think about it: If someone came to your house, stole your grandma's favorite necklace, and then wore it to your birthday party, you'd be mad. If you decided you would mass-produce your grandma's favorite necklace, sell it, and use the profits to start a scholarship in your grandma's name, you probably wouldn't be mad when you saw girls at the mall wearing it.

Often, people engaging in cultural appropriation have no idea that they're doing something wrong, because they're ignorant of the group they're appropriating from. It's totally possible for marginalized groups to engage in appropriation, too. Case in point: I was a really big No Doubt fan in high school. Once, when I was staying with my dad, I decided I wanted to wear a bindi just like Gwen Stefani. I couldn't find a bindi in small-town Ohio, where my dad lived, so I bought googly eyes, took the pupils out, and crafted a makeshift third eye. I was sporting my new bindi at the grocery store when I heard a little kid say, "Mom, what's on that girl's forehead?" The mom replied, "She's of a different religion, honey." I wasn't of a different religion, honey, and I shouldn't have been wearing that bindi. (And neither should Gwen.)

Dragging—the process of publicly shaming someone who has done something embarrassing or downright offensive. Dragging often takes the form of humor, through jokes, subtweets, memes, etc.

Ethnicity—a social group that has shared traditions. Not to be confused with **race**. Example: Latinx is an ethnicity, but Latinx people can be of any race.

Feminist—as the author Chimamanda Ngozi Adichie says, in a speech sampled in Beyoncé's song "Flawless": A feminist is a "person who believes in the social, political, and economic equality of the sexes." Lots of people misunderstand this one.

Free speech—an often-misunderstood term derived from the First Amendment of the Constitution, which protects the right to freedom of speech, press, religion, and assembly. It establishes a citizen's right to speak freely without retribution from the government, though it does not include speech that incites harm to others, making or distributing "obscene materials," and a couple of other very specific instances. It also does not extend to personal consequences for speech, which have nothing to do with the government. In other words, your mom grounding you for saying "fuck" at your grandma's seventy-fifth birthday party is not infringing on your right to freedom of speech.

Gaslighting—psychological manipulation that attempts to cause a person to question their reality or lived experience. Named after the 1944 film *Gaslight*, in which a man attempts to convince his wife that she is losing her grip on reality so that he can commit her to a mental institution and get her out of his hair, this is a favorite tactic of dictators, abusers, and bigots. A few gaslighting techniques include lying, especially when there's blatant proof of the truth; denial; turning other people against you; questioning your sanity or mental health;

and projection. Recommended reading: Lauren Duca's brilliant *Teen Vogue* article "Donald Trump Is Gaslighting America."

Gender binary—the (restrictive) idea that there are only two genders.

Gender expression—the way a person outwardly presents in terms of gender.

Hate speech—protected free speech that nevertheless disparages, bullies, harasses, or denounces marginalized groups. If you operate a hate site that promotes hate speech, you may not be committing a crime, but that doesn't mean you won't get kicked off your server.

Homophobia—anti-gay speech, behavior, or sentiment that may be suggestive or overt. Examples of homophobia range from a man's unwillingness to show other men affection for fear of being labeled gay, to media portrayals in which gay men are presented as stereotypes or as threatening/contaminating the minds of children, to two women being denied the right to adopt, to bakeries refusing to make wedding cakes for gay couples. Not all anti-gay sentiments are rooted in fear, as the suffix "-phobia" suggests, but many are.

Humanist—the identity that "devil's advocates" choose when they don't want to say they are feminists, because they feel threatened by feminism or feel feminism is excluding men somehow. Technically, the term refers to someone who privileges the human reality over a spiritual or divine being.

Intersectionality—coined by civil rights activist Kimberlé Williams Crenshaw, the idea that different identities and systems of oppression overlap and intersect. For example, a black woman experiences sexism that is often mixed with racism, while a lesbian woman experiences sexism that is often mixed with homophobia.

Latinx—a more inclusive, gender-neutral way to refer to people from Latin America. Pronounced "La-TEEN-ex."

LGBTQ(IAA)—an acronym that stands for [*clears throat*]: lesbian, gay, bisexual, transgender, queer, intersex, asexual, ally. The acronym was originally simply LGB, but as visibility of different identities and sexualities has increased, it has expanded to its current form—I've chosen to use LGBTQ in my text, but you may also see LGBT, LGBTQI, LGBTQIA.

Male chauvinism—performative or aggressive masculinity that promotes the idea that men are superior to women. The word "chauvinism" on its own refers to explicit nationalist pride/patriotism/jingoism.

Male gaze—coined by the feminist film critic Laura Mulvey in 1975, a term from film or art criticism often used to denote an oversexualized or otherwise heavily male perspective on female subjects.

Marginalized—a term used to describe a person or group of people who are oppressed in some way(s). It has more or less replaced the term "minority," which suggests the sense of being "less than" or small in number, which is not really accurate. (None of the following are small in number, for example, but they are all marginalized in various ways: low-income people, Latinx people, women.)

Meninist—a word I can't believe people really say. A troll-y ideological identity that dudes created to center conversations about gender equality around themselves. Related to **men's rights activists**.

Men's rights activist (MRA)—another thing I can't believe people really say. A reversal of the phrase "women's rights activist," this is also a troll-y ideology that dudes created to center conversations about gender equality around themselves.

Microaggression—coined by Harvard professor Chester M. Pierce in 1970, a term for the daily, casual, and often unintentionally hurtful comments that marginalized people experience from people in positions of privilege. "SWGSTBG" was comprised of the microaggressions white girls frequently use to subtly degrade black girls. Other examples include: "You're a big girl, but you have such a pretty face," "You don't *sound* Latino," and "You're not like other girls."

Misandry—the hatred of men. Also not really a thing, except in certain feminist circles, where women will occasionally say they're misandrist ironically (or mostly ironically).

Misogynoir—coined by Moya Bailey in 2010, a term that describes misogyny aimed specifically at black women. It is an intersectional way to talk about misogyny. (*Transmisogyny* is the similar principle applied to trans women.)

Misogyny—the hatred of women.

Nonbinary—generally, the quality of being defined by more than two things. In social justice contexts, someone who identifies as nonbinary doesn't identify as a man or a woman.

Oppression—the myriad ways systemic forces exert power over groups of people.

Oppression Olympics—a term used to (disparagingly) describe the competitive language that crops up with marginalized groups when comparing privileges or disadvantages. This hierarchical attitude can exist within a marginalized group or between groups.

Passing (race and/or gender)—a term most often used in the context of transgender people being identified as cisgender, and mixed-race people being identified as one race over another. Example: "My friend Joel is mixed race, but he passes as white."

Patriarchy—a sweeping system of societal norms and behaviors that contribute to inequality between men and women. Evidence of patriarchy is present in everything from rape culture to the cost of women's toiletries as compared to men's. Though patriarchy oppresses women, it enforces strict roles for men, too.

Politically correct—a negative term referring, usually, to language that protects or refuses to offend marginalized groups, often used to deride activists or progressives and portray them as overly sensitive or beholden to an imaginary establishment status quo. In the 1970s and '80s, progressives used the term to mock the idea that we should accept the status quo, but since then it has totally reversed meaning, and has been weaponized against the same people who used to say it.

Privilege—the societal advantages possessed by a group of people based on their race, class, gender, sexuality, or physical ability. This word tends to freak people out because they assume having privilege means they're a bad person or are to blame for the mistreatment of others. In reality, everyone has some level of privilege, or rather a combination of privileges. Having privileges doesn't mean you're rich, have never worked hard, or never had to struggle. It just means that there are some things you'll never have to experience or think about because of who you are.

Problematic—an umbrella term and conversation-ender that expresses, generally, that someone or something is bigoted or microaggressive. If you want to keep from being critical in any meaningful way—which you don't—you can say something is problematic. Also used when people are too shy to say something was racist, sexist, homophobic, transphobic, ableist, or otherwise bigoted.

Queer—an umbrella term for LGBT people that conveys, broadly, that someone (or something) is not heterosexual or expressing a heterosexual perspective. Since it has also been used as a slur, not everyone in the community is down with this term, so proceed with caution if you're straight.

Race—a social construct that is used to define and inhibit as well as to forge communities. Commonly, it refers to shared physical traits, culture, and especially skin color. Not to be confused with **ethnicity**.

Racism—a system of language, behaviors, and policies that oppress nonwhite people. Can be overt (**white supremacy**) or subtle and ingrained (**microaggressions**).

Rape culture—the prevailing customs and beliefs surrounding sexual assault that privilege perpetrators over victims. Mechanisms of rape culture include ideas about what types of people are rape victims, the shaming of sexual assault survivors, victim blaming, and the casual diminishment of the seriousness of the crime. It is intertwined with **patriarchy**.

Revenge porn—nude photos or media of sexual acts that are published or distributed without a featured party's **consent**, and with the express aim of harming the nonconsenting party. It's now officially illegal in many states, with more surely on the way.

Safe space—a place where visitors can be sure they will not experience **triggers**, and where their identities and experiences will be respected. (The idea of safe spaces is highly and unnecessarily controversial.) Most often used in the context of colleges and universities, but not exclusively. For example, an organization may provide a safe space for sexual assault survivors or LGBTQ students as a way to encourage those groups to share their experiences openly and comfortably.

Sexism—speech, behavior, or actions that imply or directly state that women are inferior to men, or that promote inequality.

Shaming—the act of mocking, moralizing, or insulting certain behaviors, traits, or identities. Common examples of shaming include fat-shaming, kink-shaming, and slut-shaming (see page 43).

Slacktivism—a disparaging term used to minimize someone's work/identity as an activist, often associated with internet activism, hashtag activism, or "clicktivism." Describes, basically, any kind of activism you can do while sitting on your couch, and actions that range from changing your Facebook profile photo, which is largely performative, to promoting important studies and articles or otherwise disseminating information. People use this term as a way to dismiss nontraditional forms of activism, which may or may not be effective.

Social justice warrior (SJW)—a pejorative term used to describe people who vocally advocate for social justice in order to paint them as an irrational, whiny army of crybabies who sit on social media all day. You rarely see a person self-identify as a social justice warrior. Some people may do so ironically, but I don't, because it allows critics to group activists together in order to insult or degrade them and their work.

TERF—an acronym that stands for trans-exclusionary radical feminist. The term originated in the second wave of feminism, and it describes a movement that aims to exclude trans women from feminist spaces on the grounds that they are not "real women." This is fucked up.

Tone Police—a person or people who attempt to tell you the correct way to speak about your experience, usually in order to make them more comfortable. Examples of tone policing include: "You're embarrassing me," "You're making a scene," "You're being hysterical," "Why do you sound so angry?" (see page 192).

Toxic masculinity—a term that describes how masculinity standards set for men lead to acts of aggression or violence, which may range from domestic violence to mass shootings. The harmful effects of unreachable goalposts established by the **patriarchy** inevitably seep into the world.

Transgender—a term used to describe someone who does not identify with the gender they were assigned at birth.

Transphobia—anti-trans sentiment, often rooted in fear, ignorance, or lack of exposure. Examples of transphobia include anti-trans bathroom laws and common plots in shitty comedies wherein a (usually evil, duplicitous) character is exposed as trans (*Ace Ventura: Pet Detective*, *The Hangover Part II*). (Please don't judge me for having seen *The Hangover Part II*.)

Transracial—a term popularized by Rachel Dolezal to (incorrectly) refer to someone who has changed their race. You may hear people ask, "Why can't she change her race if Caitlyn Jenner changed her gender?" The answer is kind of academic, but basically: Because race is a social construct largely related to skin color, you can't change your race. When used correctly, "transracial" is an adoption term that refers to children adopted by parent(s) of a different race.

Trigger—something that brings back memories of a traumatic incident.

Trigger warning—a preemptive note about the content of a post, article, show, or speech that signals it may contain **triggers** for some people. Frequently used with material involving sexual assault, police brutality, or abuse, but can be applied to a wide range of triggers.

Victim blaming—a strategy for explaining tragedy that falls back on things said or done by the victim of that tragedy. People often engage in victim blaming out of judgment, fear, or the desire to come up with an explanation for bad things that happen to innocent people.

White feminism—a nonintersectional branch of feminism that excludes or ignores issues faced by women who are not white, straight, cis, able-bodied, or middle class or above. Rarely self-identified.

White supremacy—a holistic, racist ideology that promotes the idea that white people are superior to people of all other races, often justified through phony biological or evolutionary explanations. Like with **patriarchy**, evidence of white supremacy may be explicit—expressions of white power or Nazism—or subtle, through standards of beauty, media representation, or the justice system. White supremacy is not always obvious to the untrained eye, or to white people who are used to seeing themselves favorably represented. This is why it's important to, as they say, stay **woke**.

Woke—a term that refers to having had one's eyes opened to societal injustice, deriving from the idea that at one time you were "asleep" and now you're awake. In the past, it was used as a kind of friendly warning among marginalized people to "Stay woke," but now people use it, inappropriately, to denote a kind of achievement or destination, ignoring the fact that there's always work to be done. "Getting woke" should be a moment on your journey, because we never stop having our eyes opened to experiences that we don't have because of our own privilege or biases.

Womanist—coined by the writer Alice Walker, a term to describe an alternative movement that seeks to broaden feminism to better cater to and include women of color.

That's all I have for now, though I'm sure I've missed something. As I said above, this is not intended as a comprehensive list of every word or phrase used in activist spaces. Language is constantly changing and evolving, and the internet only speeds up that process. Keeping track of it all may seem daunting, but it can also be rewarding. Words are linked to the power structures they represent, and using them carefully and correctly is a sign of respect, to marginalized people and to yourself. Besides, what else are you going to use when you want to speak your mind?

ACKNOWLEDGMENTS

I know I've said this before, but writing a book is freaking scary. It's also hard and draining. More often than not, throughout this entire process, I was a complete nightmare of a person. (Seriously—don't try to write a book and produce a TV pilot at the same time.) For that reason, I have a few people to thank.

First, my incredible husband, podcast cohost, and part-time tear drier, Patrick, for reassuring me at every turn, and always keeping it real, offering encouragement, making me laugh until I cry, and showering me with love. I really don't know how you put up with my shit, but I'm so thankful that you do. My parents, who gave me life (duh) and who have always believed in me and pushed me to do my best. I owe Dad for my sense of humor and the stubbornness that made many of my hilarious fails possible. Mom, your grace, poise, patience, expert-level shade, and passion for nail art are sprinkled throughout these pages; thank you for modeling the kind of woman I've always wanted to be. My little cousins, who I wish were my sisters, Danielle and Ashley: You make me proud every single day and give me a reason to work for the better world that I know the two of you will run one day.

My amazing friends: De'Lon Grant, Dylan Marron, Shamika Martinez, Michelle Buteau, Delina Medhin, Annette Roche, Alex Leo, Ceci Fernandez, Laura Turner Garrison, Erica Williams Simon, Kimberly Luskey, Jordan Carlos, Danielle Young, Francheska Medina, Grace Edwards, Meghan Tonjes, Andrew Gunadie, and Oneika Raymond, for graciously responding to novel-length text messages, showering me with GIFs, and providing the late-night laughs that kept me going.

ACKNOWLEDGMENTS

The people who made my very first book cover the cutest ever: My Glam Squad and two of the sweetest, most hardworking black women I know, Annette Roche and Delina Medhin, for keeping my edges laid, my face slayed, and my heart forever full. Superstar photographer Erin Patrice O'Brien and ultra-cool stylist Jocelyn Kaye, you're both so fun and easy to work with.

The amazing team that made this book happen and talked me off many a ledge: Brittany McInerney, your thoughtfulness, insight, and words of wisdom truly made this process fun, illuminating, and as painless as possible. Lauren Oyler, I'm convinced you're an actual superhero. You swooped in and saved my ass while never losing your cool and always being on time. Please teach me your ways. Brian Lemus, your eye and talent for design are unparalleled. My literary agent, Brandi Bowles, for never mincing words, which makes your praise that much sweeter. My manager, Kara Welker, for putting out every fire and being the ultimate gut check. My Gersh agents, Scott Yoselow and Rachel Zeidman, for always looking out for me and making me laugh.

And finally, Filthy McNasty and Kaya, the best puppies—and birth control—possible. You're still not allowed on the couch.